Sacred Healing of Marriage

DOES PRAYER MAKE A DIFFERENCE?

Timothy A. Heck, PhD

Leitourgia Press
INDIANAPOLIS, INDIANA

Copyright © 2018 by Timothy Heck, PhD.

All rights reserved. No part of this publication may be reproduced, distributed or transmitted in any form or by any means, including photocopying, recording, or other electronic or mechanical methods, without the prior written permission of the publisher, except in the case of brief quotations embodied in critical reviews and certain other noncommercial uses permitted by copyright law. For permission requests, write to the publisher, addressed "Attention: Permissions Coordinator," at the address below.

Timothy Heck/Leitourgia Press
P.O. Box 503464
Indianapolis, IN 46250
Leitourgiapress.com

Book Layout ©2017 BookDesignTemplates.com

Ordering Information: Leitourgiapress.com
Quantity sales. Special discounts are available on quantity purchases by corporations, associations, and others. For details, contact the "Special Sales Department" at the address above.

Sacred Healing of Marriage/ Timothy A. Heck —1st ed.
ISBN 978-0-578-42606-8

Library of Congress Control Number: 2018914168

Contents

Contents i

Introduction to the Problem 1

    Background of the Study 4

    Statement of the Problem 5

    Purpose of the Study 8

    Rationale 10

    Research Questions and Hypotheses 12

    Significance of the Study 15

    Definition of Terms 16

    Assumptions and Limitations 18

    Nature of the Study 19

    Design of the Study 20

Literature Review 23

    The Gottman Model 29

    The PREP Model 40

    Behavioral Marital Therapy 50

    Summary Comments on Marital Therapy 57

    Religion, Theology, Spirituality 58

and Psychotherapy..58

Background Studies on Integration..62

of Religion and Healthcare..62

Integration Models Found in the Literature 64

Ethical Issues and Concerns in...73

Faith-Based Counseling and Research...................................73

Empirical Research in Support of Integration......................76

Prayer as a Treatment Intervention 79

Prayer as a Cognitive Psychological Intervention................82

Types of Prayer and a Rationale for Scripted Prayers as a Marital Intervention..88

Conclusion..90

Methodology Research Design...93

Description of the Intervention 95

and the Control Group..95

Sampling 100

Instrumentation (DAS)..104

Data Collection Procedures..109

Data Collection and Analysis..113

Preliminary Analyses 125

Hypotheses 137
Exploratory Analyses 143
Results, Conclusions and Recommendations 149
Results of the Research 149
Limitations 159
Conclusion 161
Recommendations for Future Research 162
References 167
Appendix A 209
Appendix B 211
An Experiment in Marital Satisfaction 211
Appendix C 215
Appendix D 217

Like most of the greatest challenges in our lives, this one has exceeded my expectations in the demands it has levied on me and on my family. Since my earliest days in college, I longed for the day when I would complete my formal education at the doctoral level. In 1989, I was making progress on that goal when my ship ran off course and nearly sank on the shores of a broken life. Doubts that the journey would ever come to an end left me with little hope for the dream. Then my Lord gave to me the gift I never deserved and I will forever cherish, my beautiful wife, Margie.

She brought me hope out of my despair, friendship to fill the loneliness, love to revive my broken heart, and partnership on the quest for holiness. So, it is to you, my love, that I dedicate this work. You have accompanied me every step of the way and shored me up when weariness would have me abandon the call. This study is filled with words, but I am speechless to find the ones that would best convey all the gratitude that fills my heart and the love that burns in my soul for you. I pray our marriage will always burn with the flame of God's holiness and that we will continue to turn to Him daily in constant prayer. Your own faithfulness in prayer has been an inspiration to me in this work about the power of prayer to restore and rekindle the fire of love in any marriage that turns to our Father in heaven. My Karis, have I told you lately that I love you?

"Prayer is not asking. Prayer is putting oneself in the hands of God, at His disposition, and listening to His voice in the depth of our hearts."

—MOTHER TERESA

CHAPTER ONE

Introduction to the Problem

Marriage as an institution in contemporary culture is in a state of distress, with a risk of divorce rate reaching into the 60% range for couples planning to marry in the near future (Gottman, 1993). Research in the field of marriage and family therapy has attempted to explain this phenomenon, particularly through the study of couple interaction (Gottman & Krokoff, 1989). Validated instruments are available to assess the level of satisfaction and adjustment in a marital relationship (Spanier, 1976). A significant challenge for the marriage clinician is effecting positive change on the level of satisfaction perceived and experienced in the relationship in order to stabilize the relationship and reduce the risk for divorce (Baucom, Epstein, Sayers, & Sher, 1989; Beach, Etherton, & Whitaker, 1995; Berger & Hannah, 1999; Christensen, Atkins, Berns, Wheeler, Baucom, & Simpson, 2004; Fincham, Garnier, Gano- Phillips, & Osborne, 1995; Gottman & Notarius, 2000).

A change in marital satisfaction often hinges on a shift in the partners' ways of viewing each other in the relationship, referred to in the literature as marital sentiment (Fincham, Beach, & Baucom, 1987; Fincham & Bradbury, 1989; Fincham, Garnier, Gano-Phillips, & Osborne, 1995; Weiss, 1980; Hawkins, Carrere, & Gottman, 2002). Marital sentiment was first identified by Weiss (1980) in his evaluation of spousal reactions during marital interaction. The construct refers to a global dimension of affection or disaffection for one's spouse and the marital relationship (Hawkins et al., 2002). The sentiment is based on subjective interpretation, rather

When marital sentiment in one or both partners is negatively skewed, the potential for override in their interpretation of spousal behavior and intent is extremely high (Beach, Eterton, & Whitaker, 1995; Fincham et al., 1995; Weiss, 1980). Acting much like a filter distorting reality, the negative sentiment presents as a formidable resistance factor in marital treatment. Doherty suggested that the cognitive attributions made by partners give support for their expectations, which then influence spousal behaviors (1981a, 1981b). How individuals think about their spouses is a strong determinant of interpersonal attraction, which contributes to the partners' affective experience of the spouse and ultimately influences marital satisfaction (Montoya & Horton, 2004).

Psychotherapy has long held to the importance of effecting a change in client's cognitions as a pathway to improved psychological and interpersonal well being (deTurk & Miller, 1986; Beach, Etherton, & Whitaker, 1995; Moller & Van Zyl, 1991). The thought processes are fundamental to a person's perception of reality and serve as predictive criterion of subsequent behavioral patterns and mood tendencies.

Research has demonstrated the effectiveness of prayer as a medium for cognitive change toward optimism and increased health, at the emotional, social, and physical level (Ai, Peterson, Bolling, & Koenig, 2002; Barrett, 2001; Biggar, Forehand, Devine, Brody, Armistead, Morse, & Simon, 1999; Butler, Stout, & Gardner, 2002; Kennedy, 2002; Ladd & Spilka, 2002; Omartian & Hayford, 2003). Barrett (2001) posited that prayer has a determined effect on psychological states, specifically beliefs, opinions, desires, and emotions, and further found that individuals were more likely to make requests of God to act psychologically, rather than mechanistically in their lives.

This study attempts to explore the effect of 30 days of spousal prayer, using the Omartian prayer book series (2004a; 2004b) in the lives of Catholic and Protestant Christian married couples on their level of marital satisfaction. Given the broad and diverse range of meaning associated with prayer, a narrowing of the activity is necessary for this study in order to investigate the specific effect of Christian prayer among professing Catholic and Protestant married couples. This is not to minimize the potential efficacy of other kinds of prayer among various religious groups, which could serve as the basis for further study, however, it does facilitate a clearer exploration of the kind of prayer activity common to professing Christian couples as it relates to their relationship satisfaction. The uniqueness of this approach lies in the combination of sound psychological theory regarding cognition, reliable constructs concerning partner sentiment as a determinant in marital satisfaction, and the religious practice of prayer.

Background of the Study

The culture of this new 3rd millennium is not altogether sympathetic to marital stability (AAMFT, 2002). Stanley (2003) points to the skepticism of the culture regarding marriage, typifying a climate of apathy and fear, noting, "People have begun to shy away from marriage- not because they do not desire it or seek it, but because they fear that it is not really possible to have a lasting, healthy, and satisfying marriage" (p. 224). The literature is clear about the negative consequences for spouses and children of divorce (Amato, 2001; Bloom, Asher, & White, 1978; Hetherington & Kelly, 2002; Ross & Mirowsky, 1999; Stanton, 1997; Wallerstein, J., 1991). Nobel Laureate Gary Becker (1991) stated the condition succinctly – "The family in the Western world has been radically altered—some claim almost destroyed—by events of the last three decades" (p. 1).

The state of marriage in America is evident in the distressed effects of marital deterioration and dissolution on family members (Hetherington et al., 2002; Ross et al., 1999). Quality of life is significantly diminished by the tragedy of a marital breakup. Marriage and family therapists are challenged to find effective interventions to stop the bleeding and push back the tide of divorce. Even physical health is a casualty of marital distress (Amato, 2000; Hu & Goldman, 1990). Levenson & Gottman (1983, 1985) offer astounding findings about the deteriorated immune systems of spouses in distressed marriages and divorced individuals (Gottman, 1999; Gottman & Levenson, 1992). Far reaching are the negative effects of the breakdown of a marriage for individuals, communities, employers, and the nation.

Religiosity has been found to be positively correlated with marital satisfaction and improved dyadic adjustment (Blummel, 1992; Bock & Radelet, 1988; Burgess & Cotrell, 1939; Hunt & King, 1978; Jenkins, 1992; Mahoney, Pargament, Jewell, Swank, Scott, Emery, & Rye, 1999; Wilson & Filsinger, 1986). By exploring the relationship between the religious activity of praying for one's spouse among Christian couples and the couples' level of satisfaction in their marriages, this study proposes to discover yet another effective intervention for improving relations and stemming the tide of divorce.

Statement of the Problem

Counseling is concerned with the process of change. Whether at the behavioral, emotional, or cognitive level, the focus of most psychological treatment is on how to affect the greatest degree of change desired by the client with the least intrusive and costly intervention (Nichols & Schwartz, 2004). Resistance represents a great challenge to psychological treatment. When resistance is present in married couples the result is frequently treatment failure and subsequent divorce (Gottman, 1999). Hahlweg and Markman's (1988) meta-analysis assessed the effect size of behavioral marital therapies as .95, representing an improvement rate of 44%. By adding unpublished dissertation studies, Shadish, Montgomery, Wilson, Bright, and Okwumabua (1993) obtained a smaller effect size of .74, representing an improvement rate of only 35%. These odds for success are not impressive and have shown limited change over the past decade, as Gottman (1999) notes:

> To summarize, after taking a hard look at relapse rates, our current best estimate is that for about 35% of couples marital therapy is effective in terms of clinically significant, immediate changes, but that after a year about 30-50% of the lucky couples who made the initial gains relapse. (p. 5)

Marriage and family therapists are always in search of new and improved methods for dismantling the resistant factors and engendering motivation and hope into their spousal clients to effect enduring change for the better.

Some psychotherapists are inclined to accept the resistant state of the client(s) as indication of a failed marriage, resigned to the inevitability of a divorce. Others attribute the resistance to characterological issues that might warrant an Axis II diagnosis, such as an Avoidant Personality Disorder (Baucom, Shoham, Mueser, Daiuto, & Stickle, 1998; Berger & Hannah, 1999; DSM-IV, 1994). Still others will opt in favor of individual therapy in hopes of promoting some positive influence on the attitudes and motivation of the partners in the marriage. While these and other similar approaches may be appropriate at times, the result can be individual change at the expense of the marital relationship (Gottman, 1999).

Integrative couples behavior therapy seeks to promote change and break down resistance through interventions targeted at the clients' cognitive states (Baucom & Epstein, 1990; Baucom, Epstein, Daiuto, Carels, Rankin, & Burnett, 1996; Baucom, Epstein, Sayers, & Sher, 1989; Christensen, Atkins, Berns, Wheeler, Baucom, & Simpson, 2004; Christensen & Heavey, 1999; deTurck & Miller, 1986; Fincham & Bradbury, 1989; Gottman, 1999; Jacobson, Christensen, Prince, Cordova, & Eldridge, 2000). A positive in the marital partners' cognitive states increases their mutual affect, motivation for relational improvement, and rekindles hope for the marriage. Prayer is recognized in the literature as applicable to life issues and is used by many people as a source of supportive encouragement in the face of ongoing distress (Butler & Harper, 1994; Chibnall, Jeral, & Cerullo, 2001; Gruner, 1985; Koenig, 1997; Koenig & Larson, 2001). Butler, Stout and Gardner (2002) have demonstrated the value of prayer as a ritual to aid couples in the resolution of conflict in the marital relationship. Research in the field of medicine advocates for prayer as an intervention to raise patient attitude toward optimism (Dossey, 1993; Koenig, 1997, 2003; Koenig & Cohen, 2002). What is missing is the study of how consistent praying on the part of a married couple, for themselves and each other around relevant marital issues and needs, over a predetermined and relatively brief period of time can affect the cognitive and affective state of those spouses.

Purpose of the Study

The sentiment of spouses in marriage, including their attitude and motivation, is the target for the proposed treatment. Assisting a person in altering his perception of the marriage partner, particularly when the relationship has deteriorated into a significant condition of distress is a formidable task. The corroded interaction of the couple leads to a negative feedback loop in which the individual falls into a confirmation bias, believing the worst about the partner and looking for that which confirms the belief (Markman & Hahlweg, 1993). Further, the negative perception leads to a negative interpretation of the behavior of the partner, as if to say, "She's doing this on purpose!", as well as a limited capacity to recognize positive behavior when it does actually occur in the partner (Gottman, Murray, Swanson, Tyson, & Swanson, 2002; Gottman & Notarius, 2000). His reaction is to behave in a way that feeds into the negativity of their interaction and the loop continues (Gottman, 1999).

Perception, or to use Weis's (1980) terminology – marital sentiment – seems to be the problem that feeds the resistance. The key to effective intervention will include an altering of this sentiment into a more positive one, reminiscent of former days in the couple's early relationship. Courting couples are quite optimistic with their sentiment toward each other, willing to give each other the benefit of the doubt in most cases (Gottman, Coan, Carrere, & Swanson, 1998). Their emotional bank account (Gottman, 1999), a metaphor for the couple's friendship, runs high with positive sentiment, evident in feelings, attitudes or cognitions, and behaviors toward the partner (Hawkins, et al., 2002). In a positive feedback loop, the couple engages in behaviors, which are kind, loving, and considerate with each other that subsequently build the account balance higher. When the inevitable argument or negative behavior takes place, the partners, now filled with positive sentiment, either overlook the negativity or even re-frame it in a more positive light, i.e. "I know she didn't mean that. She's just having a bad day" (Hawkins et al., 2002).

Marital satisfaction is not static; rather, it is a dynamic dimension of the couple's relationship that responds to effective interventions. This study approaches the question of whether and to what extent daily spousal prayer among professing Catholic and Protestant Christian couples over a thirty day period by both partners in the marriage affects the level of marital satisfaction for the couple as measured by a valid and reliable instrument, as compared to a control group undergoing a cognitive affirmation intervention (Gottman, 1999) over the same period of time and measured by the same instrument. Secondarily, the work attempts to address the question of the difference in marital satisfaction change over the 30-day period among the two groups identified as Catholic and Protestant married couples that participate in the study. Although the literature in the field of marriage and family studies does not yet support a distinction between these two denominations within Christianity, such a distinction is found in the literature in the field of theological studies (McDowell & Stewart, 1983; Rayburn, 2001; Tan, 2003). This second aspect explores the sometimes subtle, yet distinct differences between Christianity as practiced by Catholic married couples and Protestant married couples.

Rationale

In recent years the lines separating spirituality and psychology have become blurred (Clinton & Ohlschlager, 2002; Koenig & Cohen, 2002; Koenig & Larson, 2001). Drawing upon the extensive literature that recognizes a strong link between religion/spirituality and mental health, practitioners in the field are more open to the exploration of bridges that can span the two disciplines (Chamberlain & Hall, 2000; Koenig, 1998; Larson,

Swyers, & McCullough, 1998; Plante & Sherman, 2001). This is not a dabbling in witchery or the dangling of crystal beads in the face of clients, rather a scholarly approach to the integration of psychology and theology toward finding models of effective intervention for clients in personal and marital distress.

With a membership well into the tens of thousands, the American Association of Christian Counselors (AACC) is evidence of the increasing number of qualified clinicians making an effort toward such integration. Their mission statement reads,

> AACC is committed to assisting Christian counselors and the entire 'community of care,' licensed professionals, pastors, and caring church members with little or no formal training. It is our intention to equip clinical, pastoral, and lay caregivers with Biblical truth and psychosocial insights that ministers to hurting persons and helps them move to personal wholeness, interpersonal competence, mental stability, and spiritual maturity. (AACC, 2004)

By blending a religious activity like Christian prayer, demonstrated in the literature to have a positive impact on cognitive outlook consistent with optimism, this study attempts to explore more specifically whether engagement in certain kinds of spousal Christian prayer (Omartian, 2004a, 2004b) over a determined period of days can have a significant effect on married partners' marital sentiment as measured by the construct known as marital satisfaction (Ai, Peterson, et al., 2002; Hawkins, et al., 2002).

Praying regularly brings peace to many people and helps them find better ways to cope with the painful parts of their lives (Koenig, 2003). Most hospitals, even non-religiously oriented ones, have a chaplain or even a pastoral department within its personnel to provide care and spiritual support to patients and their families during a time of crisis and suffering. Crises and the distress that usually accompanies such a time of loss, trauma, or tragedy, often bring people to their knees in search of God to help in ways beyond their own capacity. It has been said, "There are no atheists in foxholes!", a reflection of this truism that the threat of a crisis compels us to search for answers and/or comfort from one who is greater than ourselves.

Research Questions and Hypotheses

This research aimed at three questions relevant to marital satisfaction. First, whether 30 days of daily prayer by marriage partners results in a statistically significant improvement on marital satisfaction measured by the DAS dyadic adjustment scores? Second, whether 30 days of daily affirmation by marriage partners results in a statistically significant improvement on marital satisfaction measured by the DAS dyadic adjustment scores? And third, whether the average change from baseline to follow-up was significantly greater for the treatment-prayer group couples from the control-affirmation group couples? Given the differences apparent among professing Catholic and

Protestant Christians (McDowell & Stewart, 1983), the study also explored possible differences in outcome from the treatment intervention with the two groups. The baseline DAS score was compared between Protestants and Catholics participating couples. In an effort to add value to the pool of interventions utilized in the service of marital stability, improvement, and maintenance, the focus of the work is on the integration of the religious activity of prayer.

The measures for the study included one dependent variable and two independent variables. The dependent variable was the marital adjustment score on the Dyadic Adjustment Scale (DAS). The DAS was measured on a continuous scale with a theoretical range of possible values of 0 to 151. Two independent variables were measured in the study. The first independent variable is time, which was measured on nominal scale with two categories, baseline—prior to 30 days of daily spousal prayer, and follow-up—after 30 days of daily spousal prayer. The second independent variable is type of intervention, which was measured on nominal scale with two categories, scripted daily Prayer versus scripted daily Thoughts.

Given the diverse understandings of prayer outside of the Christian religion, this study only included those couples that professed to be either Protestant or Catholic Christians. As stated previously, other studies among married couples in other religious groups in which prayer has wider or different meanings is warranted, but not the focus of this work. The null and alternative statistical research hypotheses are can be stated as follows:

Three statistical hypotheses will be tested in this study. Note, H_0: represents "null hypothesis" and H_a: represents "alternative hypothesis".

Hypothesis 1:

H_0: The average DAS score is the same at baseline and follow-up for the treatment- Prayer group.

H_a: The average DAS score at follow-up is higher than the average DAS score at baseline for the treatment-Prayer group.

Hypothesis 2:

H_0: The average DAS score at follow-up is higher than the average DAS score at baseline for the affirmation-control group.

H_a: The average DAS score is the same at baseline and follow-up for the affirmation- control group.

Hypothesis 3:

H_0: The average increase in DAS score from baseline to follow-up is the same for the prayer-treatment and affirmation-control groups.

H_a: The average increase in DAS score from baseline to follow-up for the prayer- treatment group is greater than the average increase in DAS score for the affirmation- control group.

Significance of the Study

The significance of the study is a contribution to the effort in improving distressed couples' marriage satisfaction by demonstrating one possible means of affecting a change in their cognitive marital sentiment toward each other (deTurck & Miller, 1986; Fincham & Bradbury, 1989; Fincham, Garnier, Gano-Phillips, & Osborne, 1995; Gottman, 1999). This study will specifically look at using a series of previously published prayers (Omartian, 2004a; 2004b) over a 30-day period. Although issues of randomization and control are considerations as possible limitations, which will be addressed later in this paper, there is still merit in evaluating how prayer changes thoughts, feelings, and behaviors among marriage partners.

Given the diverse array of innovative and imaginative interventions at the disposal of professionals working in the arena of marital therapy, it should not be surprising to discover that a spiritual discipline dating back to the days of antiquity might make a noticeable difference as well (Nichols & Schwartz, 2004; Foster, 1992). Dr. Larry Dossey (1994) goes so far as to suggest that prayer is "one of the best kept secrets in modern medicine" despite its ancient origins. As an internal medicine physician, former chief of staff of Medical City Dallas Hospital, and a past co-chair of a panel with the Office of Alternative Medicine at the National Institute of Health (NIH) Office of Alternative Therapy, Dr. Dossey is anything but a fanatic out to convert the world to his form of religion, but he is quite serious about the efficacy of the practice of prayer in the lives of his patients.

Dossey's work is complemented by other studies of significant relevance that support the potential of distant intercessory prayer for medical healing (Kennedy, 2002). Although controversial in nature, particularly with regard to whether such research assumes the existence of a supernatural being, it remains that the findings lend toward optimism about prayer's efficacy. To ignore such evidence and disregard the possible effects for mood elevation, cognitive improvement, sentiment increase, and marital satisfaction would be to exclude a powerful element for marital intervention. In light of the vast number of theoretical models developed over the past 50 years to explain marital and familial dysfunction, it behooves us to explore any model that might better answer the difficult questions about marital distress.

Definition of Terms

A discussion of marital distress presumes a basis for the construct of marital satisfaction. Marital satisfaction is generally viewed as a result of the combined partners' reported level of positive feelings toward and thoughts about each other (Gottman, 1998; Montoya & Horton, 2004; Moller & Van Zyl, 1991; Beach, et al., 1995; deTurck & Miller, 1986). Certain activities correlate to the affective and cognitive domains, particularly communication patterns and spousal behaviors. When communication is poor between marriage partners, usually their marital satisfaction corresponds. When behaviors are more negative, self-centered, or hurtful in some way, a downward trend in satisfaction is predictable.

The interaction that takes place in the marriage is often referred to as a dyadic process, not unlike when any two individuals engage in some kind of relationship. When assessing the quality of the relationship it is critical to gain some measure of the participants' representation of the relational experience. Spanier (2004) refers to this as "a measure of the quality of adjustment to marriage and similar dyadic relationships" (p. 1).

Marital sentiment has been recognized in the literature as a construct of the married partners' overall assessment of the spouse (Weiss, 1980; Hawkins, et al., 2002; Gottman, 1993; 1999). While affection or disaffection is the key result of the sentiment, cognitive evaluation is the primary determiner (Montoya & Horton, 2004; deTurck & Miller; 1986; Moller & Van Zyl; 1991). The thoughts in the mind of the partner about the spouse will drive the affective response toward that person. The combination of the thoughts and the feelings represents the marital sentiment or perception toward the spouse in the marriage. Reality, then, truly is in the mind of the beholder, contingent upon the cognitive and affective dimensions of the individual.

Prayer is a commonly understood activity in which an individual attempts to engage the Divine Presence of God, usually involving spoken or unspoken expressions of praise, thanksgiving, confession, or petition. With some exceptions, it is normally associated with a process of personal surrender out of a helplessness to control some or many aspect(s) of one's life (Foster, 1992). "To pray," writes Emilie Griffin (1984), "means to be willing to be naïve" (p. 5). This apparent acknowledgement of incapacity motivates the individual to a kind of abandonment into the hands of God, in the hope that he can do what the individual cannot.

Assumptions and Limitations

Social science research requires sensitivity to the nature of the constructs under study, which do not usually fall into easily defined or measurable categories (Sprenkle & Moon, 1996). Undertaking a study of marital satisfaction and prayer warrants such a level of sensitivity in order to appreciate the delicate nature of the elements for discussion. People's lives and relationships can never be reduced to simple dimensions to be examined, tested, re-tested, and analyzed. Respect for the complexity of the persons, the relationship, and the spiritual act of prayer must guide the researcher in any such exploration.

Several limitations apply along those lines around social science research with human participants. The first challenge will be soliciting the participation and full cooperation of the sample couple participants. Due to the quantitative methodology to be employed in the study, a sample of no less than 53 couples will be required to authenticate the findings (Bernard, 2000). It will also be difficult to ensure that the participating couples will actually engage in the daily ritual of reciting the two prayers on behalf of the spouse. Although tracking in a journal on a daily basis will be employed to assist with this limitation, it does not eliminate the possibility that some participants will fail to complete the 30-day cycle of praying.

The mortality rate, couples dropping out of the study for any number of reasons, will also be a challenge that may limit the research, particularly if the size of the sample drops close to or below 45 couples (Sprenkle & Moon, 1996). Controlling for extraneous variables that may contribute to an increase or decrease in marital satisfaction over the 30 days is always a factor in this type of study (Bernard, 2000; Creswell, 2003; Greenstein, 2001). Maturation itself could account for a certain amount of central tendency in the data from the Time 1 and Time 2 testing on the DAS (Spanier, 1976).

Nature of the Study

This is a study relevant to the field of marriage and family therapy, with a focus on marital dynamics and treatment interventions. Because of the inclusion of prayer as an intervention with married partners, the study of theology, spirituality, and religiosity is also addressed in this work. Marriage is the domain to be explored. Satisfaction is the dimension under examination. Prayer is the treatment intervention postulated. And positive effect is the anticipated result of the study.

While it remains to be seen whether such an effect will emerge and of what significance it will be, it is appropriate that research be continually conducted in this field to find better, more effective treatment modalities and intervention models in the discipline of marriage and family therapy.

Design of the Study

This study employs a quasi-experimental nonrandomized control group pretest-posttest design (Leedy & Ormrod, 2001). The single group, though stratified into Catholic and Protestant samples, will undergo a pre-experimental evaluation with the DAS, followed by a 30 day period in which they will recite the Omartian (2004a, 2004b), and finally undergo a second evaluation with the DAS following the prayer period. The control group will also undergo a baseline evaluation with the DAS, followed by a 30-day period in which they will recite scripted thoughts concerning their spouse (Gottman, 1999). If the treatment couples' DAS scores at the conclusion of the prayer period are improved at a statistically significant level beyond that of the control group couples, it may be possible to attribute the benefit to the daily prayers by the partners. Of course, the model is limited in that other explanations for the change could be proposed, however, this is an introductory study that warrants further research to better discern how prayer might serve as an intervention for cognitive change, improved sentiment, and increased marital satisfaction.

CHAPTER TWO

Literature Review

Statistical data reveals a staggering divorce rate in the United States. The Census Bureau states, "The fastest growing marital-status category [over this twenty-five-year period] was divorced persons. The number [of] currently divorced adults quadrupled from 4.3 million in 1970 to 17.4 million in 1994" (Saluter, 1996, p. vi.). In 1950 three out of every four households were married couples, representing 78 percent of the population, while in 2000 that number declined to 52 percent (U.S. Census Bureau, 2000, p. 148).

Religion plays a significant role in the lives of Americans, 95% of who express a belief in God (Shafranske, 1996). Of relevance to this study is that 84% of adults believe God can be reached through prayer (Mahoney, Pargament, Jewell, Swank, Scott, Emery, & Rye, 1999). Religious observance has been linked to higher marital satisfaction in classic and recent studies (Burgess & Cottrell, 1939; Dudley & Kosinski, 1990; Locke, 1951; Wilson & Musick, 1996).

Facts about the increasing divorce rate may have little bearing apart from associated research about the effects of both divorce and marital distress on family members. The consequences of divorce are recognized as severe on the mental and physical health of both partners, as well as the children in these distressed and broken families (Ardell Wellness Report, 2000; Bloom, Asher, & White, 1978; Cherlin & Furstenberg, 1991; Jacobson & Gurman; Gottman, 1998).

Stanton asserts,

As the researchers have gone to press with their work and produced an enormous literature, one of the most consistent findings is that men and women do markedly better in all measures of specific and general well-being when they are married compared to any of their unmarried counterparts. Married couples are healthier—physically and mentally- and they live longer, enjoy a more fulfilled life, and take better care of themselves (and each other). This has been shown consistently over decades, but it is rarely mentioned in the popular debate on the family. One of social science's best-kept secrets is that marriage is much more than a legal agreement between two people. Marriage truly makes a difference in the lives of men and women. (1997, p.73)

A recent report from family scholars, including Doherty, Gottman, Markman, Popenoe, Stanley, and Wallerstein (Institute for American Values, 2002), presents 21 conclusions from the social sciences in support of marriage as an institution. One conclusion is that marriage increases the likelihood that fathers have good relationships with their children. Amato and Booth (1997; 2001) found that children of divorced or never-married parents see their fathers less frequently and have diminished relationships with their fathers than children of intact marriages. Divorce is associated with certain psychological risks for children, though not serious mental illness (Hetherington & Kelly, 2002). Divorce and unmarried childbearing are shown to increase poverty for both children and mothers in such conditions (McLanahan, 2000; Blank, 1997; Rank & Hirschl, 1999; Bianchi, 1999). One study of 500 repeat juvenile offenders found that marriage reduced the offense rate by two-thirds as compared to those who did not marry or who had failed marriages (Laub, Nagin, & Sampson, 1998).

Wallerstein (1995) depicts the prevailing skepticism toward marriage in the culture when she tells of participating in a monthly meeting with dozens of her friends and colleagues in the field. In the context of their sharing about their work, Wallerstein reported that she was interested in learning about what makes a good marriage. She further expressed her desire to conduct some research into couples that were in successful marriages and determine the characteristics and qualities that led to their success. Upon asking the group if they would be interested in joining her in the venture they broke out in laughter. Wallerstein was dumbfounded by their reaction. She explains, "Their laughter bore undertones of cynicism, nervousness, and disbelief, as if to say, 'Surely you can't mean that happy marriages exist in the 1990s. How could you possibly believe that?'" (1995, p. 3).

Yet as problematic as divorce is to family members, chronic marital dissatisfaction and conflict offers little more relief for married partners (Amato & Booth, 2001; Baucom, Shoham, Mueser, Daiuto, & Stickle, 1998). Vandewater and Lansford (1998) note "a growing number of studies have found that even among families who have never experienced divorce, conflict between parents has a negative impact on children's psychological adjustment" (p. 323). It is difficult to determine whether the parental conflict is more or less damaging to the child(ren) than divorce, somewhat like choosing suicide by drowning or a drug overdose.

These data clearly support the need to prevent and remediate marital distress. Society is desperately in need of resources to strengthen the marriage institution and withstand the onslaught of damage this age-old enterprise has undergone in the past thirty years. The list of treatment options available to marriage counselors is vast, drawing frequently from theoretical positions taken more from intuitive introspection than objective analysis (Baucom et al., 1998; Gottman, 1998). It is too tempting for the clinician to adopt an individualized approach that approximates more of a "fly-by-the-seat-of-the-pants" style, than a solidly researched model of intervention designed to effectively assess and treat marriages in distress.

Given the number and diversity of marital treatments available to the practitioner, consideration of three models relevant to the proposed study is given herein, chosen specifically for their similarity as forms of behavioral marital therapy and because of the research basis underlying each model, as well as the outcome studies to validate each model's effectiveness as a treatment modality for couples (Gottman & Levenson, 2002; Halford, Sanders, & Behrens, 2001; Christensen, Atkins, Berns, Wheeler, Baucom, & Simpson, 2004). Wallerstein's (1995) idea to research the characteristics of good and distressed marriages has been undertaken over the last ten years (Gottman & Notarius, 2000; Wallerstein & Lewis, 2004).

The first model under review is identified with John Gottman, researcher with the Department of Psychology at the University of Washington and founder of The Gottman Institute. Next the author will offer a review of the Prevention and Relationship Enhancement Program (PREP), developed out of the research work led by Howard Markman and Scott Stanley at the University of Denver (PREP, 2004). Finally, a review of the behavioral couple therapy model in its traditional and integrated forms will be undertaken (Christensen, Atkins, Berns, Wheeler, Baucom, & Simpson, 2004; Christensen & Heavey, 1999). Each review will include a brief overview of the key features of the treatment approach, as well as highlights of the empirical research in support of the model.

This study proposes spousal prayer as an intervention for marital improvement. In support of such a technique, this paper will first examine the literature for evidence of integration in the fields of religion, theology, spirituality, and psychotherapy. Background studies on the relationship of religion and healthcare will serve as a backdrop for further exploration of prayer as a treatment for psychological and marital problems. Specific integration models relevant to psychology and marital interaction will necessitate a brief look at spiritual direction, pastoral counseling, and spiritually oriented psychotherapy. Despite significant shifts in the culture around some of these issues, it remains controversial to blend the two worlds of religion and psychology, so we will include herein an overview of ethical issues and concerns relevant to faith-based counseling and research, offering empirical support for integration models in the field.

The final portion of this literature review will examine prayer as a treatment intervention, highlighting key elements around resistance factors and cognition as pertinent to marital interaction and distress that contributes to overall dissatisfaction. Given that prayer is put forth as the treatment of choice in this work and given that prayer has such diverse meanings and connotations in the literature, the rationale for certain types of prayers to use with married partners will be offered.

This review will conclude with summary comments that set the stage for the methodology employed in this unique study of spousal prayer among professing Catholic and Protestant Christian married couples.

The Gottman Model

Gottman's (1999) curiosity about marital distress and breakdown led him, not to the clinical office or even the library, but to the laboratory in order to better discern the factors contributing to such a condition. Regarding the existing methodologies for classifying marriages, he noted in 1993, "most of these classifications of marriages were not based on direct observation of how couples behaved, but rather they were based on self-report data concerning beliefs, life styles, or interaction patterns" (Gottman, 1993b, p. 6). Rather than taking his cues from what the clients said about their marriage, he set out to take a direct path to the relationship through observation of the actual marital interaction in a laboratory setting (Bakeman & Gottman, 1997; Gottman, 1999; Gottman & Notarius, 2000).

A Mathematical Model of Marriage

Gottman (Gottman, Murray, Swanson, Tyson, & Swanson, 2002) comments on his research-oriented model:

> In our view, the field of marriage research is in desperate need of theory. Without theoretical understanding of key processes related to marital dissolution or stability, it will be difficult to design or evaluate adequately any new

interventions. Personally we have the most respect for theories that are mathematical. We believe that scientific progress will be facilitated by mathematical models. (p. xi)

Interestingly, James Murray is a mathematician whose work intrigued Gottman and resulted in the formation of a research team in 1990 to examine marital process, out of which emerged a mathematical model of marriage (Gottman, Murray et al., 2002). Gottman and Murray now teach a graduate-level seminar at the University of Washington, jointly sponsored by the applied mathematics and psychology departments, bringing graduate students in the two fields together (Gottman, Murray et al., 2002). He (Gottman, Murray et al., 2002) notes, "The mathematicians have learned to become consultants, guided by James Murray, and the psychologists have learned to formulate their ideas more formally, guided by John Gottman (p. xiii).

Through the use of videotaping of marital interaction and sophisticated coding schemes, Gottman et al. (1992) have been able to study marital processes with effective reliability (Bakeman et al., 1997). Gottman and Levenson (1992) studied 79 couples through videotaped observation of three conversational interactions, which were then reviewed with the spouses for them to rate their feeling state using a dial pointer over a 9-point scale with a typical Likert scale from extremely negative to extremely positive to gain the affect ratings. The complexity of Gottman's research designs poses some threat to the replicability potential. He also tends to drain the sample by overusing the data set for additional post hoc studies. The couples from this study were re-contacted four years after the initial assessment, using two marital satisfaction questionnaires, a measure of physical illness, and several items considered relevant to measuring divorce potential among the couples. Using the Rapid Couples Interaction Scoring System (RCISS) (Krokoff, Gottman, & Hass, 1989), the couples in the sample were classified into regulated and nonregulated categories with 42 in the former category and 31 in the latter.

Gottman's development of these sophisticated coding schemes for his research with couples raises some questions around validity in that his own testing instrument may drive the findings in the studies, a problem that could be resolved through replicated work by other researchers in the field. Coding schemes, however, are not widely found in the literature, perhaps in part due to the timely and complicated design process involved. By definition, the regulated couples were those whose speaker slopes were more positive than negative. Among the findings in this particular research was a significant MANOVA group effect, $F(5, 66) = 2.80$, $p < .05$, for variables of the cascade model used by the authors as an explanation for the deterioration of the marriages of the couples who divorced, considered divorcing, and separated during the intervening four years. The results of this study contributed heavily to Gottman's theory about a cascading effect toward divorce among couples that are unable to regulate emotionality effectively in their relationships.

Several concerns are evident in the study, including the relatively small sample, the selection of the sample from a college city like Bloomington, Indiana, the significant interval of time between Time 1 and 2 testing, as well as the potential for a number of contaminating variables to affect the couples' marriages during the four-year interval.

By designing and implementing simple interventions the team was able to study and analyze the dynamic effects on the marital system. One notable phenomenon from their work is that negative codes in a marital interaction coding system are more likely to be negatively correlated with couple satisfaction and predictive of divorce than positive codes are to be positively correlated with couple satisfaction and predictive of marital stability (Gottman & Notarius, 2000). Most of the studies utilized a methodology involving videotaped observation of married couples interacting around conversational dialogue, conflict work, and informal interaction in an apartment laboratory setting (Gottman & Krokoff, 1989; Gottman & Levenson, 1992; Gottman & Notarius, 2000). Using three major coding systems, the Marital Interaction Coding System (MICS) (Weiss & Tolman, 1990), the Couples Interaction Scoring System (CISS) (Gottman, 1979), the Specific Affect Coding System (SPAFF) (Gottman & Krokoff, 1989), and the Rapid Couples Interaction Scoring System (RCISS) (Gottman et al., 2000) the researchers analyzed the taped interactions. The Cohen's kappa for the affect codes are comparable to those in other studies (Gottman, 1979; Schaap, 1982).

Gottman and Levenson

Gottman and Levenson (1992) used a similar methodology for gaining physiological, behavioral, and self-report data in a synchronized manner with a sample of 73 couples from 1983 to 1987. The raters used a 15-minute conversation in which the couples attempted to resolve a major issue of conflict in their relationship. With the use of the coding system they found the ratio of positive to negative speaker codes during the conflict resolution interaction was about 5 to 0 (Gottman & Levenson, 2002). This finding led to the conclusion by Gottman that not all negative behavior in marital interaction is equally corrosive. The behavior found to be most damaging to the relationship consists of criticism, defensiveness, contempt, and withdrawal (Gottman, 1994; 1999; Jacobson, Gottman, Gortner, Berns, & Shortt, 1996), referred to by Gottman as the Four Horsemen of the Apocalypse, a metaphorical biblical reference to the end times. As the metaphor strongly implies, when these behaviors are present with increasing frequency, the relationship is experiencing significant distress that will manifest in relationship dissatisfaction (Gottman, 1999).

Withdrawal, or stonewalling (as Gottman prefers to call the behavior), on the part of the husband was related to physiological arousal (Levenson, Carstensen, & Gottman, 1994). A common pattern in which the wife pursues for conflict resolution and the husband withdraws in a stonewalling fashion may be better understood as each spouse's effort to repair the damaged relationship, as well as the husband fleeing to safer ground where his body can recover (Gottman & Levenson, 1992; Gottman, 1999; Gottman & Notarius, 2000). Although the behaviors are well-intentioned, the subsequent effect for the marital partner is usually a further deterioration of sentiment and cognitive perception.

The Core Triad of Balance

A cycle of conflict and distancing, in which the distressed couple cascade toward divorce, finds the partners helplessly attempting to repair the severed relationship. Gottman's theory proposes that the partners nurture the relationship with turning toward behaviors, leading to positive sentiment override (Hawkins, Carrere, & Gottman, 2002). If the proportion of turning toward to turning away behaviors becomes too distorted, the result is a trend toward negative sentiment override (Gottman, 1998; Hawkins et al., 2002). Sentiment represents the partners' perceptions, cognitions, and feelings toward the spouse. As an unstable dimension of the relationship, sentiment is influenced by the couple's interaction. When the friendship is strong, the positive sentiment spills over to absorb the potential disastrous effects of any negative behavior, but negative sentiment precludes the partners from recognizing even the positive efforts of the spouse in the deteriorated marriage. The couple's proverbial emotional bank account becomes depleted and an increasing negativity characterizes the partners' cognitive states toward each other, the marital history, and their future together (Fincham, Garnier, Gano- Phillips, & Osborne, 1995; Gottman et al., 1989; Gottman, 1993a).

Gottman (1999) refers to this dynamic as the "core triad of balance" in marriage. Building on the general systems theorists he looked into the "balance of positivity and negativity in the couple's interactions, assuming that every relationship is a system that develops its own balance or stable steady states, with respect to the ratio of positivity and negativity in behavior, perception, and physiology" (Gottman, 1999). Promoting the notion that the partners bring to every marital interaction a set of uninfluenced stable steady states in behavior, thought, and physiology, Gottman and Levenson (2002) found that the positive/negative ratio in interactive behavior during conflict resolution is at least 5 to 1, as noted previously, in stable, happy marriages, whereas in marriages headed for divorce the positive/negative ratio is only .8 to 1, so that there are 1.25 as many negatives as positives. The negative behaviors observed in the study represent Gottman's (1999) four horsemen.

The Sound Marital House

According to Gottman (1999) the two elements vital for a good working marriage are an overall level of positive affect and an ability to reduce negative affect during conflict resolution. The researcher (Gottman, 1999) summarizes his treatment model by saying,

> These two empirical facts give us the basics of marital therapy: To create lasting change in troubled marriages, interventions need to enhance the overall level of positive affect in both non-conflict and conflict contexts, and teach couples how to reduce negative affect during conflict by accepting one another's influence. (p. 105)

Gottman's Sound Marital House (1999) views the marriage from the foundation of marital friendship up to the expression of that relationship through meaningful rituals of connection (Gottman, 1994). This identifiable friendship is at the core of his model. When this core begins to melt down, the marriage itself is headed for potential disaster. Couples who divorce have sustained considerable damage to the essential quality of their friendship (Gottman & Levenson, 2002). Subsequently, they find themselves locked in gridlock over perpetual issues of their relationship, often rooted in the partners' personalities (Gottman, 1994). The irony is that the personality trait that once may have manifested itself as an attraction to the partner has now become a source of irritation in which the cognitive evaluation of the same behavioral tendencies reaps a negative affect. The wife who once thought her husband was attractive because of the neat manner in which he dressed is now filled with negativity and contempt toward him because of all the money he spends on new clothes and the time he spends getting ready in the morning. The same trait is manifesting itself somewhat differently, but the problem can also be characterized as a change on the part of the wife in how she cognitively evaluates certain behaviors of order in his personality.

In support of the model are several longitudinal studies, including one that originated in 1983 in Bloomington, Indiana, using 197 couples in the sample with four-year follow-up over a 14 year period (Gottman & Levenson, 2002). The results of that study give strong support to an analytical process for determining factors present in relationships predictive of divorce. The study isolated two patterns of affect regulation in couples headed for divorce. The first pattern is an emotionally inexpressive one that is low in both negative and positive affect (Gottman & Levenson, 2002). The second pattern is an emotionally volatile one that leads to an attack-defend pattern for the couple (Gottman & Levenson, 2002). Their conclusions were that the emotionally inexpressive pattern will predict later divorce while the emotionally volatile attack-defend pattern will predict earlier divorce (Gottman & Levenson, 2002). The dependent variable in the research is the length of time a divorcing marriage will last before the actual divorce. Two criticisms of the study are the researchers' decision to use a rectangular distribution in their effort to attain an equal distribution of marital satisfaction among the couples, and their employment of post hoc analyses of their data (Gottman & Levenson, 2002).

Treatment Interventions in the Model

Intervention for Gottman (1999) is an outgrowth of the research findings. Given the potential damage caused by the Four Horsemen of criticism, defensiveness, contempt, and withdrawal (stonewalling), therapists are strongly admonished to point out such behaviors for the couple through a direct intervention (Gottman, 1993a, 1998, 1999). Through the use of videotaping and playback review in treatment, clinicians are able to process the tapes with the couples and facilitate a therapeutic process of finding the partners' intended conversation that was lost in the fight (Gottman, 1999; Gottman et al., 2002). The author-researcher depicts the underlying conversation as revolving around a dream that is now hidden within the conflict (Gottman, 1999). Therapy involves an unpacking of the fight so as to uncover the dream, dismantling the negativity within the couple's interaction.

While attempting to reduce the negative exchange, specifically the Four Horsemen, the Gottman clinician will also explore ways to assist the couple in rebuilding their essential friendship (Gottman, 1999). These interventions rebalance the positivity and negativity in the couple's interactions. One such intervention is Gottman's (1999) Seven Week Course in Fondness and Admiration. Using a cognitively-based model (Beck, Rush, Shaw, & Emery, 1979; Baucom, Epstein, Sayers, & Sher, 1989) for altering thought patterns and subsequent affect, the assignment challenges partners to think about their spouse in a more positive light. For example, on day one the partners are asked to concentrate on the thought – "I am genuinely fond of my partner." They are also given a task each day to complete, such as, "List one characteristic you find endearing or lovable."

In an effort to reduce the negativity in conflict interaction and avoid gridlock, several interventions are used to improve the couple's skills in dealing with both solvable and perpetual problems. Recognizing the power of startup in a problem discussion, Gottman (1993b) stresses the need to teach partners, particularly the wives in light of their tendency to initiate the discussion on problem issues, to do so in a softened manner (Gottman, 1999).

One of the more critical interventions recommended by Gottman (Gottman & Levenson, 1992; Gottman, 1999) is assisting couples in soothing during an escalated discussion in which they experience a condition known as Diffuse Physiological Arousal (DPA) (Gottman & Levenson, 1992). The physiological symptoms associated with DPA or flooding (Gottman, 1999) include increased heart rate, rapid breathing, sweating, and other features common to an arousal of the autonomic nervous system. Given the stronger tendency among males to experience DPA as an extremely uncomfortable state, this phenomenon gives some explanation for the withdrawal or stonewalling tendency among males in couple interaction (Gottman & Levenson,

1992; Gottman, 1993b, 1998). Teaching the couples methods for self and other- soothing is a central part of the marital treatment.

Summary Comments on Gottman's Model

Gottman is to be commended for his vast research efforts in the field of marital studies. His contributions provide clinicians with effective tools for intervention emerging out of reliable data and trustworthy analysis. Any serious marriage and family therapist will profit from his work and likely discover the accuracy of his findings in the lives and interactions of most marital clients.

Although his theory is based on solid research, the interventions lack the support of longitudinal data in reliable research settings. Future studies to better determine the effectiveness of the Gottman (1999) interventions with couples over longer periods of time will help to substantiate the treatment model. Such outcome research (Sprenkle & Moon, 1996) will either verify the effectiveness of the approach or assist those in the field in finding better ways to help distressed couples in marriage.

The PREP Model

PREP is an acronym for the Prevention and Relationship Enhancement Program (Markman, Stanley, & Blumberg, 1994), the outcome of over 20 years of research at the University of Denver. Promoted by the authors as "one of the most extensively researched programs for couples ever developed" (Markman et al., 1994, p. 2), the model focuses on a twofold approach of educating couples on the factors associated with marital breakdown and the development of skills to prevent such from occurring in their relationships (PREP, 2004). Where Gottman's model is somewhat weak on outcome research, PREP has extensive involvement with the military, the Catholic Church, various Protestant churches, and some international associations, all of which have made valuable contributions to the effectiveness of the model in practical application settings (Markman et al., 1994; Hahlweg, Markman, Thurmaier, Engl, & Eckert, 1998; Halford, Sanders, & Behrens, 2001).

History and Background

The beginnings of the PREP research extend back over 30 years to the research work of Howard Markman, Clifford Notarius, and John Gottman at Indiana University (Birchler, Weiss, & Vincent, 1975) investigating the etiology of marital distress. Of particular interest to the team was the communication patterns characteristic of the distressed couples as compared to more satisfied couples. During his residence at Indiana University, Markman (1981) began a longitudinal study to test his hypothesis around using the communication variables distinct among the distressed couples, as opposed to the nondistressed couples, to predict later marital distress and divorce. Using the empirical research from these studies, Markman (Markman et al., 1994) founded his prevention program to help couples develop the more effective communication skills characteristic of non-distressed marriages.

Markman is joined at the Center for Marriage and Family Studies at the University of Denver by others, notably Frank Floyd, Scott Stanley, and Susan Blumberg (as cited in Hahlweg & Jacobson, 1984). Through workshops and various training sessions Markman et al. (1994) disseminate the results of their research and train clinicians in the techniques and strategies for helping couples. The researchers also offer their own couples' workshops for married couples to receive first-hand evaluation and treatment from the authors in a weekend format (PREP, 2004).

The PREP research has been supported by National Institute of Mental Health, National Institute of Health, and National Science Foundation grants (Markman et al., 1994). The program has undergone a number of revisions over the past 25 years, reflecting the current research (Fraenkel, Markman, & Stanley, 1997).

As early as 1979 Markman applied the model in a premarital counseling context to determine the effects of the training for couples after their marriage. Some recent work by the research group on marital satisfaction and divorce predictions based on pre-engagement cohabitation has contributed to the controversial issue around cohabiting couples' risk for divorce (Kline, Stanley, Markman, Olmos-Gallo, St. Peters, Whitton, & Prado,

2004). The study in question was part of an ongoing project assessing the efficacy of the PREP program in a premarital context (Kline et al., 2004). Participating couples ($N = 306$) were recruited through the religious organizations that provided their wedding services and random assignment was made to one of three premarital training programs. One hundred thirty-six couples from the larger sample were included in the cohabitation study, meeting the criterion of being able to produce dates of cohabitation prior to marriage, not having been married at the first assessment, being able to read English, and entering a first marriage (Kline et al., 2004). The couples visited the laboratory before marriage and before their premarital training, as well as after premarital training and marriage. The Danger Signs Scale, an instrument with adequate validity and reliability (Johnson, Stanley, Glenn, Amato, Nock, & Markman, 2002), was used to assess relationship characteristics predictive of marital distress in the study. The Danger Signs are the negative behaviors observed in couple interaction, which have a deteriorating effect on the couple's satisfaction levels, comparable to the Gottman Four Horsemen (1979, 1993a, 1993b, 1999). These four behaviors are given the labels of escalation, invalidation, negative interpretations, and withdrawal or avoidance (Markman, Renick, Floyd, Stanley, & Clements, 1993). ANOVAs or multivariate ANOVAs (MANOVAs) using the General Linear Model routine of SPSS were used to analyze the data in the study, supporting earlier research on cohabitation and couple interaction.

Negative interaction ratings using the Danger Signs Scale were available for the couples from before and after marriage, allowing for a 3 (cohabitation type) x 2 (gender) x 2 (time) ANOVA to be conducted, which revealed a significant main effect of type of premarital cohabitation, $F(2, 105) = 6.36$, $p < .01$. Comparisons also demonstrated that the before engagement group ($M = 1.56$, $SD = 0.35$) reported higher levels of danger signs than the after-engagement group ($M = 1.38$, $SD = 0.29$), $t(67) = 2.39$, $p < .05$, $ES = .57$, and the at- marriage group ($M = 1.36$, $SD = 0.28$), $t(89) = 3.33$, $p < .01$, $ES = .71$. The main effect of time approached significance, $F(1, 105) = 3.90$, $p = .05$, $ES = .16$, with the frequency of premarriage danger signs ($M = 1.40$, $SD = 0.33$) being less than the number of postmarriage danger signs ($M = 1.46$, $SD = 0.41$) (Kline et al., 2004; Magdol, Moffitt, & Caspi, 1998). The study demonstrated that cohabiters are at higher risk for physical violence than daters. In addition, the Kline et al. (2004) study found that married couples that had lived together prior to marriage displayed more negative and less positive problem-solving and support behaviors than their non-cohabitating premarital counterparts. Like Gottman, the PREP researchers are prone to re-use data sets in post hoc analyses, a practice acceptable in research, but not without concern (Sprenkle et al., 1996).

This kind of research has afforded the authors a hearing at both the popular (Markman et al., 1994; Stanley, Trathen, McCain, & Bryan, 1998) and legislative levels, with Stanley being asked to give testimony before the Committee on Finance,

Subcommittee on Social Security and Family Policy in the United States Senate on May 5, 2004 (Stanley, 2004) on the benefits of a healthy marriage.

Theory Underlying PREP

While numerous factors have been shown in the literature to increase the risk of marital failure, including neuroticism (Kelly & Conley, 1987), premarital cohabitation (Bumpass, Martin, & Sweet, 1991; Thomson & Colella, 1992), physiological arousal prior to problem- solving discussions (Levenson & Gottman, 1983; 1985), dissatisfaction with partners' personality and habits (Fowers, Montel, & Olson, 1996; Fowers, 2000), and low or differing levels of education (Bumpass et al., 1991), to name a few, the PREP model targets those factors that are both dynamic in nature and have a causal quality in the development of marital distress that leads to divorce (Stanley, 1997).

These dynamic factors are selected for treatment because of their potential to respond favorably to intervention and include the negative communication patterns, conflict negativity, withdrawal tendencies, unrealistic cognitions and expectations, as well as low levels of commitment to the marriage (as cited in Berger & Hannah, 1999). The theory postulates that the optimism characteristic of premarital couples quickly erodes in the face of the negative process employed in handling basic life problems (Hahlweg et al., 1988; Halford et al., 2001; Markman, et al., 1994) and leaves the couple weighing out the constraints of their commitment that still have a holding power on the relationship (Stanley & Markman, 1992). Left with a disintegrated perspective (Halford et al., 2001; Baucom et al., 1989) of the marriage, past, present, and future, the couple cascade quickly toward separation and divorce.

Outcome research on versions of PREP have been conducted by various researchers in different countries with varying results. The results can be interpreted as in support of prevention efforts for marriage or as illustrative of the ways in which selection effects can convolute interpretation of effects in outcome studies (Stanley & Markman, 1998). In one of the most extensive longitudinal studies on PREP, couples who participated in the program before marriage had less negative interaction, more positive interaction, lower rates of relationship aggression, lower combined rates of breakup or divorce, and higher levels of relationship satisfaction up to five years following the training (Markman, Floyd, Stanley, & Storaasli, 1988; Markman et al., 1993). Due to differential attrition and the probable wearing off of the effect over time, the differences between controls and PREP couples after five years, however, are equivocal.

Another longitudinal study of a German version of PREP by Thurmaier, Engl, Eckert, and Hahlweg in 1993 (as cited in Stanley, Markman, Prado, Olmos-Gallo, Tonelli, St. Peters, Leber, Bobulinski, Cordova, & Whitton, 2001) showed a divorce rate of 3% in the treatment group as compared to 16% for the control couples over a five year period. Couples were not randomly assigned in this particular study, although the control group shows high external validity in its reflection of what couples often experience in their premarital training in Germany.

Stanley (1986) began a study of commitment in 1980, exploring the construct as a measure of satisfied couples. Building on commitment theory, which identifies the related constructs of personal dedication and constraint commitment, Stanley and Markman (1992) developed the Commitment Inventory as an instrument to measure commitment levels in married partners. The sample ($N = 141$) were drawn from church groups, graduate programs in psychology, and community contacts of research assistants on the team. The participants were given 16 items on commitment, using a 7-point Likert scale for responses. A minimum threshold of a coefficient alpha of .70 was used for each of the 10 subscales, all of which met the established criteria. A second study (Stanley et al., 1992) used a new sample for a reassessment of the internal consistency of the subscales on the CI and to evaluate the correlation of the measure with other validated measures on the construct. While the authors recognize the need for more sophisticated measures on commitment, the CI does show promise for both research and clinical settings, particularly when used in conjunction with marital satisfaction measures (Stanley et al., 1992).

The current versions of PREP, and particularly the Christian version, take advantage of Stanley's research on the subject to help develop and strengthen couples' level of mutual dedication in the relationship (PREP, 2004; Stanley et al., 1998). A key finding in the validation studies on the CI is the correlation of a pattern of low dedication commitment and high constraint commitment with low marital satisfaction.

Because of the stress the authors of PREP place on premarital intervention for couples, most of the outcome research centers around the premarital model, as opposed to treatment with married couples in distress (Stanley et al., 1998; Stanley et al., 2001). Although Markman and Stanley (PREP, 2004) are quick to predict similar results with married populations, the scant amount of data available raises some question as to its crossover application in the treatment stage with more seriously distressed couples.

Treatment Interventions in the Model

The program and techniques of PREP are designed to be delivered in a behavioral marital treatment model (Berger et al., 1999). The primary treatment objectives include the development and supervised practice of constructive communication interaction and conflict management skills, the expression of marital beliefs and expectations, the enhancement of fun, friendship, and spiritual connectedness for intimacy, providing the couple with a set of ground rules bilaterally agreed-upon for handling disagreements, and the development of skills to better understand and improve their mutual level of commitment (Markman et al., 1994; Berger et al., 1999; PREP, 2004).

The PREP model lends itself to a broad spectrum of applications, including the professional counseling practice, the pastoral counselor, chaplaincy, and even certain non- professional groups (PREP, 2004). An intervention stressed more than any other in the model is the Speaker-Listener Technique (Markman et al., 1994) in which the couples are coached to both express their message and listen to each other in a non-defensive manner, then give a summary of the message heard. Ironically, this particular intervention is criticized heavily by Gottman and Notarius (2000) as a communication pattern that is both awkward and uncharacteristic of stable and satisfied married couples. Like many marital treatment interventions, the tool shows effectiveness within the treatment session, yet may lack the potential for application in the real life setting. This is certainly an area where additional outcome research would be extremely beneficial (Sprenkle et al., 1996).

Summary Comments on the PREP Model

Markman et al. (1993, 1994) are to be commended for their research efforts in the field of marital studies. They offer a model that has strong empirical support (PREP, 2004) and is relatively easy to learn and implement. Their emphasis on prevention is distinctive and borne out in the outcome studies they have conducted to date. The simplistic nature of the model is appealing to the practitioner who prefers not to delve too deeply into the etiological background of the couple's problems. This, of course, may also constitute a criticism of PREP in that it might lead the therapist to overlook relevant material contributing to the couple's present state of distress. As a prevention model, PREP stands out as worthy of consideration, however, in terms of marital treatment it may lack the comprehensiveness of the Gottman model. More longitudinal studies are needed in order to evaluate the true effectiveness of prevention programs like PREP (Christensen et al., 1999).

Behavioral Marital Therapy

Behavioral marital therapy, also known as behavioral couples therapy (BCT) or traditional behavioral couple therapy (TCBT) is supported by extensive research (Jacobson et al., 2000) and its efficacy has been repeatedly demonstrated in a series of randomized clinical trials (Baucom et al., 1998; Christensen & Heavey, 1999; Jacobson & Addis, 1993). BCT characterizes marital satisfaction and maladjustment in reinforcement terms. Couple satisfaction is a correlate of a positive ratio of reinforcement to punishment and dissatisfaction is a correlate of a negative ratio. The treatment for the condition constitutes an increase in the level of positive reciprocal exchange of behavior between the partners, as well as skill building in communication and problem solving without negativity (Christensen et al., 1999, 2004).

Since the early work of Jacobson and Margolin (1979), a modified approach, known as integrative behavioral couple therapy (IBCT) or cognitive behavioral marital therapy (CBMT) has developed with a greater focus on cognitive aspects of marital distress (Jacobson, Christensen, Prince, Cordova, & Eldridge, 2000). The primary aim of behavioral couples therapy is helping spouses change in light of their partners' complaints, necessitating a participative interactive process between the partners (Jacobson et al., 1979). In the integrative approach (IBCT) a key strategy is to assist spouses in accepting traits of their partners that were previously deemed negative and unacceptable (Christensen et al., 2004; Jacobson et al., 2000). This dimension of the model incorporates a cognitive element of the treatment recognized in the literature as a critical factor in marital dysfunction warranting treatment (Fincham, Garnier, Gano-Phillips, & Osborne, 1995; Gottman, 1993a, 1999, Hawkins, Carrere, & Gottman, 2002; Montoya & Horton, 2004).

Both models are based on social learning principles reliant on interventions designed to alter behavior in the couples' interaction. The shift toward the cognitive aspects of the spouses arose in part due to the reduced impact of BCT over time (Hahlweg & Markman, 1988). Particular attention has been given to the cognitive process around the explanations that spouses give for partner behaviors and occurrences in the marriage (Baucom, Epstein, Daiuto, Carels, Rankin, & Burnett, 1996).

The Role of Cognition in Marital Processes

The dimension of cognition as a factor in the development and maintenance of marital distress and maladjustment is derived largely from Beck's (1976) and Ellis' (1962) cognitive theories of abnormal behavior. Because of the relative nature of partner perceptions concerning marital events and partner behavior, a major task of integrative behavior couple therapy is to help spouses become more discriminating of their observations and their subsequent cognitions in order to minimize distortions (Fincham, Beach, & Baucom, 1987; Montoya et al., 2004).

Spouses in distressed marriages are more likely to attribute negative events in the relationship to the personality or behavior of the partner (Baucom et al., 1996a; Baucom, Epstein, Rankin, & Burnett, 1996b; Hawkins et al., 2002; Stanley et al., 1992). Fincham and Bradbury (1989) demonstrated the importance of attributions and efficacy expectations for marital satisfaction in their study of 130 couples over a twelve month period, assessing for attributions regarding partner behavior with an efficacy expectation scale developed by the authors, the Locke-Wallace Marital Adjustment Test, and a demographics questionnaire at Time 1 and Time 2 (12 months later). The results of the study showed both the reliability of the measure and the relative importance of the construct for marital satisfaction.

Validating the earlier work of Weiss (as cited in Vincent, 1980) Hawkins et al. (2002) contributed to an understanding of the integral relationship of partner cognitions with sentiment override with their study of couples ($N = 96$) who participated in a marital interaction laboratory session, along with Buehlman and Gottman's (as cited in Gottman, 1996) Oral History Interview. The researchers employed regression analyses of spouses' marital bond to predict their rating of the partners' expressed affect in the oral history interview and the marital interaction. The results offered support for the belief that sentiment override serves as a perceptual filter through which wives, in particular, evaluate their husbands' behavior (Hawkins et al., 2002). Wives' marital bond scores, a measure of the spouses' perceptual biases about each other and the relationship (Carrere, Buehlman, Gottman, Coan, & Ruckstuhl, 2000), are correlated to sentiment override only up to a certain level of toxicity for the wives, however, the scores are predictive of husbands' positive affect. The gender specific finding concerning wives' greater vulnerability to sentiment override is consistent with past research on the construct (Helgeson, 1994).

Communication Patterns in Distressed Couples

The most common complaint of distressed couples that seek out marital treatment is poor communication (Hahlweg, Revenstorf, & Schindler, 1984; Sher & Baucom, 1993; Baucom et al., 1998). Negativity is much more pervasive in the communication patterns of distressed couples (Gottman, 1999; Sher et al., 1993). Marital therapists consider communication the most damaging relationship problem characteristic of presenting couples (Geiss & O'Leary, 1981; Walsh, Baucom, Tyler, & Sayers, 1993).

Bakeman and Gottman (1986, 1997) found, for instance, that if the overall likelihood of a husband communicating negatively with his wife is .20 and increases to .50 because her prior communication to him was negative, then the investigator could surmise that there is a sequential pattern in which the wife's negative communication influences the husband to counter in a negative fashion. BCT therapists instruct couples in how to express themselves without blame and attack toward the partner, as well as in the use of active listening skills (Christensen et al., 1999).

Because of criticisms that BCT research focuses on communication patterns of distressed couples primarily around conflict and problem-solving (Baucom & Epstein, 1990), more recent approaches (Gottman, 1998, 1999, Walsh et al., 1993) focus equally on partner communication on non-conflictual exchanges and friendship building dialogue. Baucom et al. (1990) demonstrated that distressed couples receiving a form of communication training which focuses on the sharing of emotions feel closer and more trusting toward each other after treatment.

Treatment Intervention in the Model

Motivation of the partners to engage in the exchange of positive behaviors is the primary aim of behavioral marital therapy. The treatment often begins with helping the spouses to identify those positive acts they would like the other to perform which would increase their sense of support and care, an intervention formalized by Stuart (cited in Thompson & Dockens, 1975). The invocation of each partner's participation in a unilateral change of behavior toward the spouse has the potential to break the cycle of negativity in the marital interaction.

As the amount of positive behaviors continues, the partners' cognitive perspectives are influenced respectively (Christensen et al., 2004) with a feedback loop created that feeds the movement toward increased marital satisfaction (Bakeman et al., 1997; Gottman, 1999). In ICBT the therapist further challenges the couple to concentrate on only spousal behaviors that are deemed positive (Baucom et al., 1990) so as to elicit an elevation in the cognitive evaluation of the spouses.

Of course, IBCT therapists use many cognitive restructuring strategies to modify various kinds of dysfunctional thought patterns true of the partners. In order to change assumptions, attributions, and expectations the marriage therapists may engage the partners in a challenging approach where they are challenged to reconsider the rationale and logic of their standards, expectations, and thoughts about the partner (Christensen et al., 1999; Fincham et al., 1989, 1995). In an effort to alter the context in the therapy session, the therapists shifts the partners from adversarial confrontation to collaborative engagement. Wimberly (1998) showed significant improvement among randomly assigned couples assigned to an IBCT treatment, as compared to 9 wait-list couples at the end of treatment.

Summary Comments on the Behavioral Model

More studies have been conducted on BCT than on any other couple therapy (Christensen et al., 2004). Hahlweg and Markman (1988) conducted a meta-analysis on 17 studies of BCT with the result being an overall effect size of 0.95. They also found that the results of the treatment were stable over a period up to one year. Dunn and Schwebel (1995) found a weighted mean effect size of 0.79 at post treatment and 0.52 at follow-up (average 8.75 months) on 11 published studies between 1980 and 1993 with 13 BCT treatment groups.

Both TBCT and IBCT have demonstrated effectiveness in marital satisfaction improvement, usually experienced earlier in treatment than later, although IBCT has shown some greater impact over its traditional predecessor (Christensen et al., 2004). Research has also shown that husbands tend to benefit more from TBCT than IBCT (Christensen et al., 2004). One of the criticisms of most outcome studies is the fact that they are normally conducted prior to treatment and at the end of treatment, with minimal data on the change during the actual course of the therapy (Jacobson, Christensen, Prince, Cordova, & Eldridge, 2000).

Summary Comments on Marital Therapy

The three models of marital treatment have demonstrated validity in the effort to assist distressed couples. The discerning therapist is well advised to become familiar with the constructs identified in each model as they contribute to an overall understanding of the marital interaction process. None of the models identified need be utilized exclusively in marital treatment. Certainly, more research is needed to best understand what type of intervention is best suited to particular couples based on their relationship dynamics and presenting issues (Jacobson & Addis, 1993). However, the value of the research in the field of marital studies has grown extensively over the past 30 years, adding to a greater clinical precision in marital therapy practice.

PREP stands out as an excellent prevention model that has promising prospects for couples considering marriage (Schilling et al., 2003). Perhaps more states will look seriously at requiring such preparatory programs for couples applying for a license to marry. If a license to drive necessitates a level of study, preparation, and examination, can it be rightfully argued that marriage deserves anything less? The enhancement program could have positive implications for remediation against marital breakdown and divorce for participating couples.

It is encouraging that these past 30 years has witnessed an elevation of marital research in the literature on psychology (Baucom et al., 1990; Berger et al., 1999; Bloom et al., 1978; Carrere et al., 2000). Attitudes and beliefs about marital interaction have been challenged by valid and reliable research in the field. The long-standing belief that satisfied couples are characterized by a reciprocal principle according to which they merely exchange positive behavior has been shown much less true than the principle of negative behavior reciprocity (Gottman, 1993a). Research has moved past the examination of mere behavior, and now recognizes the value of cognition in the process of marital interaction (Fincham et al., 1989, 1995).

Given the negative and disruptive effects of divorce on the health of the individual family members and, arguably, society itself, the hope remains that continued research such as the one underway in this study will provide greater clarity in the effort to understand how to restore the "for better" part of the marital vows when the partners are entangled in the "for worse" snare of distress.

Religion, Theology, Spirituality and Psychotherapy

Politics and religion are considered topics prone to create controversy in almost any conversation. The typical response is avoidance of these charged matters, yet this question begs the discussion of an apparent relationship between psychology and religion in the literature. That such a relationship exists is evident from a review of the sociological history on how mental health problems have been treated over the centuries

(Alexander & Selesnick, 1966; Koenig & Larson, 2001; Zilboorg, 1941). The current relevancy of this discussion is supported by a decade of statistical data indicating that 96% of people living in the United States believe in God, more than 90% pray regularly, 69% are members of a church, and 43% have attended a church, synagogue, or temple within the past 7 days (Gallup, 1995; Princeton Religion Research Center, 1996).

Alexander and Selesnick (1966) point out that one of the first hospital institutions established to care for the mentally ill was part of the religious order of the Church in Jerusalem in AD 490. A Franciscan monk named Bartholomaeus in the 13th century wrote a work depicting the etiology of mental illness from natural, rather than supernatural causes (Kroll, 1973). The Church in Spain further established asylums for the insane in the 15th century that provided better care than their State-based counterparts (Latourette, 1953). Of course, during the 15th century and for the next 200 years, religion entered the dark ages of its practice with mental illness, attributing so much of the symptomatology to demonization, resulting in the torture and execution of thousands of the innocent ill (Zilboorg, 1941). At the turn of the 19th century William Tuke, a Quaker in England, founded the York Retreat for the mentally ill, offering a medical-based approach to treatment and care, called "moral treatment" (Koenig et al., 2001; Taubes, 1998). This has been cited (Taubes, 1998) as the first organized form of psychiatric care in this country. The chaplaincy movement also accompanied the moral treatment of the Quakers in America. Samuel Woodward wrote in the 19th century, "By our whole moral treatment, as well as by our religious services, we try to inculcate all of that which is rational" (as cited in Koenig et al., 2001, p. 68). Interestingly, Woodward would found the Association of Medical Superintendents of American Institutions for the Insane, today known as the American Psychiatric Association. The American Journal of Psychiatry was preceded by the American Journal of Insanity, the official publication of Woodward's organization (Koenig et al., 2001).

This is the history prior to the divorce brought about by Freud's early views of the religious neuroses associated with mental illness (as cited in Strachey, 1962). The force of that opinion shaped the thinking of the scientific community for decades to come, supported by the foundational work of Albert Ellis (1980, 1988), who "argued that the less religious people are, the more emotionally healthy they will be" (as cited in Koenig et al., 2001, p. 67). Carl Jung (1933), in his own rebuke of religion, wrote:

> During the past thirty years, people from all the civilized countries of the earth have consulted me. I have treated many hundreds of patients, the larger number being Protestants, a small number Jews, and not more than five or six believing Catholics. Among all my patients in the second half of life—that is to say, over 35—there has not been one whose problem in the last resort was not that of finding a religious outlook on

life. It is safe to say that every one of them fell ill because he had lost that which the living religions of every age have given to their followers, and none of them has been really healed who did not regain his religious outlook. (p. 229)

The negativism of the early writers has had a dominating influence on philosophical thought in the field of psychology over the past century (Koenig, 1998; Koenig, McCullough, & Larson, 2001).

It is into this cauldron of skepticism that Fuller Theological Seminary founded the first doctoral program with an integrative emphasis, offering a Christocentric training curriculum in psychological training (Maloney, 1995). The Rosemead Graduate School of Professional Psychology, established as the first freestanding Christian doctoral program of its kind, soon thereafter, joined Fuller Seminary in a novel attempt to challenge the prevailing attitude in the academic community of psychology (Maloney, 1995; Pike, McMinn, & Campbell, 1997). However, the climate of the professional world was matched by the skeptical climate of the religious community who feared the secularism of psychology. Fuller and Rosemead found themselves in a high-pressure quandary, as depicted by the following comment: "The faculties of both of these programs were pressed by their secular colleagues with the view that one could not be intelligent (scientific, academically sound) and religious at the same time. They were also pressed by their Christian communities with the view that one could not be Christian and a psychologist (humanist, scientist) at the same time (Pike et al., 1977, p. 279).

Given that over 90% of the American population claims a belief in God, according to Hoge (as cited in Shafranske, 1996), an apparent bias in secular graduate programs in psychology toward overly religious applicants and a growing recognition among Christian churches for better care for the mentally ill and emotionally disturbed, the rationale is set for integrative training programs and a bridging of the gap between the sacred and the secular.

Background Studies on Integration of Religion and Healthcare

Studies conducted between 1950 and 1970 did not produce results conducive to a support of the integration of religion and healthcare (Sanua, 1969). More recent studies, however, have challenged the methodologies of the earlier research that relied on convenience samples of college students and psychiatric patients (Koenig et al., 2001). A number of the older works failed to control for covariates and used college student samples characterized by an immaturity regarding religion. Koenig et al. (2001) offer a different perspective on this period in the literature, "Inverse cross-sectional relationships between religion and mental health may mean that being religious increases mental distress, or it may mean that mental distress increases religiousness as persons seek comfort and solace from these beliefs" (p. 70).

Current reviews of the literature demonstrate a linkage between religion and physical health (Koenig & Cohen, 2002; Thoresen, 1999). Noteworthy is Rayburn's (2001) use of the term "theobiology" to reflect an interconnection with theology and biology. One meta-analysis of the literature (McCullough, Hoyt, Larson, Koenig, & Thoresen, 2000) found a strong odds ratio of religious involvement and mortality (OR = 1.29), suggestive that the religious has 29% greater odds of survival during a follow-up period than the less religious. Cardiovascular health benefit has been identified in the literature as a significant health outcome in relation to religiosity (Lawler & Younger, 2002; Levin & Vanderpool, 1989).

Powell, Shahabi, and Thoresen (2003) have put forth a critique of the reviews on the linkage of religion to physical health, arguing previous reviews relied on too many studies in which bias and confounding are minimized. Powell et al. (2003) offer a review utilizing a levels- of-evidence approach, evaluating 9 hypotheses using only "studies that meet minimally acceptable methodological standards" (p. 36). Although less optimistic about their findings, Powell et al. (2003) conclude that "a relationship between religion or spirituality and physical health does exist" (p. 50).

Integration Models Found in the Literature

A marriage between these two fields is founded on the premise of a revelation from God in the form of nature, referred by theologians as "general revelation", and in the form of Scripture, referred to as "special revelation" (Brown, 1981; Henry, 1977; McDowell & Stewart, 1983). Although the focus of this paper is on Christian religion, theology, and spirituality, many of the concepts have a broader application to other religions. Islam, for instance, is built on the belief in one God, Allah, and the visions or revelations the prophet Muhammad received from Allah, which are recorded in the Qur'an (McDowell et al., 1983). The practice of integration of psychology with religion is nowhere more developed as systematically and empirically, in more recent years, as is found in the Christian traditions (Clinton & Ohlschlager, 2002; Ripley & Worthington, 1998; Maloney, 1995). This distinctive understanding of divine revelation that includes nature fosters the appreciation among Christian psychotherapists for truths supported in research efforts. Jones (as cited in Clinton et al., 2002) make a strong case for research found within Scripture in support of current methodologies, citing an intriguing example of how a counselor might incorporate the two sources for illustration.

Research can affirm biblical truth by confirming a biblical principle through general revelation. For example, a client was distraught over his divorce. He had not wanted it, but his wife refused to consider reconciliation. As he struggled with the issues, he discovered a book detailing a longitudinal study on the effects of divorce on children (Wallerstein, 2000). The research confirmed the troubling social effects of divorce on children and identified specific difficulties including such issues as loss, change, conflict, and a sense of betrayal. The client's counselor used the information to affirm biblical truths and help the client anticipate potential problems that his children might face in the future. (as cited in Clinton et al., 2002, pp. 651-652)

The wise clinician and researcher attempting to bridge faith and psychology will examine all relevant claims with equal measure and rigor, remaining open to new understandings of the world that will enlighten his perspective for the ultimate benefit of the client.

In understanding the rationale behind integrative efforts and Christian based counseling in general, it is normally framed in an attempt to relieve human suffering (Anderson, Zuehlke, & Zuehlke, 2000; McMinn, 1996; Clinton et al., 2002). Compassion is a quality highly esteemed and promoted in Christian communities and applauded among leaders in churches and parachurch organizations (Collins, 1998; Crabb, 1993, 2001; Moon, 1994; Nouwen, 1972). Given the universality of pain and suffering, human service professionals are recognized as instrumental in both the alleviation of the distress and alteration of the client's perspective of the distressing factors of his life (Anderson et al., 2000; Crabb, 2001).

One additional point regarding this practice of integration bears mention, that being the somewhat artificial seams distinguishing the various sub-disciplines within integrated models. Because no one model of Christian therapy can be found in the literature, it is a challenge to determine how spiritual direction, pastoral counseling, and spiritually-oriented psychotherapy might work out in practice (Worthington, Karusu, McCullough, & Sandage, 1996). This finding, however, is not inconsistent with what is commonly found in the clinical practice of psychotherapy as the theoretical models are applied in clinical contexts (Sprenkle & Moon, 1996). With this introduction to integration theory it will now be worthwhile to explore three particular models for practice application evident in the literature.

Spiritual Direction

Fewer people, even regular attending church members, turn to the institutional church for guidance and counsel during times of personal difficulty and distress (Sperry, 2003; Stairs, 2000; Steere, 1997). This may be a reflection of a loss of confidence in institutional religion and a consumer-oriented culture that prefers to find help in more privatized settings, a need met by the rise of psychotherapy services (Lescher, 1997; Nichols & Schwartz, 2004). Spiritual direction is a form of help drawn from the rich traditions of orthodox Christianity, yet being practiced in more para-church settings by representatives from Catholic, Greek Orthodox, Episcopal, and even Protestant denominations (Sperry, 2003; Ruffing, 2000; Edwards, 2001).

Spiritual direction goes by many names, including spiritual guidance, spiritual companionship, and spiritual friendship. Thornton (1984) gives the practice the simple definition, "the application of theology to life of prayer" (p. 1). While therapy typically revolves around the function of symptom reduction and pain relief, spiritual direction focuses on the individual's spiritual movement toward a more intimate relationship with God (Stairs, 2000). The relationship between the director and client, usually referred to as the directee, is a collaborative one that incorporates dialogue, narrative, Scripture, prayer, and silence (Ruffing, 2000). Leech (1977) calls the practice "the cure of souls...a seeking after the leading of the Holy Spirit in a given psychological and spiritual situation" (p. 34).

A study of 315 ($n = 315$) spiritual directors, psychologist members of the Christian Association for Psychological Studies (CAPS), and psychologist members of the American Psychological Association (APA) to ascertain and compare the participants' mental health and spiritual values Christian psychologists "share many values with spiritual directors" (Howard, McMinn, Bissell, Faries, & VanMeter, 2000, p. 312). Using a randomized sample from the three representative groups, the participants were administered two questionnaires to measure mental health values and the central values and perspectives of the classic figure of spiritual direction from the middle ages, St. John of the Cross. The 315 responses yielded a return rate of 54%, including 134 spiritual directors, 72 from the APA sample, and 109 from the CAPS sample. Chronbach alpha coefficients for the 10 themes from the first questionnaire (Jensen & Bergin, 1988) scale ranged from .72 to .92, a good indicator of item consistency in the survey (Bernard, 2000). A series of one-way analyses of variance (ANOVA) was used in combination with a priori t test contrasts to examine the hypotheses. Howard et al. (2000) found that most psychologists share many of the viewpoints common among spiritual directors and further, that Christian psychologists hold values concerning spirituality similar to those derived from St. John of the Cross. Despite the methodological issue with using a survey developed for this study alone, the St. John of the Cross values survey, this is suggestive of a high level of similarity across the fields of spiritual direction and psychology.

Pastoral Counseling

The second discipline in which integration of psychology and theology or religion is identified is pastoral counseling. Clergy are in a position of leadership that frequently leads to perceptions among their parishioners that they are also a source of wisdom and guidance for dealing with life's problems (Stone, 1999). Those who present to pastors, ministers, priests, and pastoral counselors raise concerns and issues similar to those of psychological provider clients (Stone, 1999; Wise, 1983).

The rise of the counseling movement in Christian circles led to the establishment of graduate degrees, usually Master of Arts or Master of Science level, in the field of counseling, pastoral counseling, or spiritual psychotherapy (Maloney, 1995) as a way to be better prepared to meet the growing demands in the church for the counseling service. An example of the increasing attention devoted to pastoral counseling at the graduate level, Denver Seminary now offers five graduate degrees in counseling, including a Master of Arts in Counseling that is preparatory for state licensure, a Master of Arts in Counseling Ministries, a Master of Arts in Counseling Ministries/Chaplaincy, a Master of Arts in Youth and Family Ministries/Counseling, and a Doctor of Ministry in Marriage and Family Therapy (Denver Seminary, 2004).

As noted, it is not easy to discern the differences in the professional or licensed professional who earned a degree from such a graduate program and the pastoral counselor who earned a parallel degree from the same or a similar institution, as both are focused on symptom relief and resolution of the presenting problem(s) (Sperry, 2003). Some say the distinctions are artificial and indistinguishable apart from the parameters associated with the setting itself, such as an intake process, session fees, insurance filing, and other professional versus church-oriented practices (J. Craig, personal communication, November 12, 2004).

Pastoral counselors do not generally engage in the psychotherapy of personality disorders and personality change (Sperry, 2003). In most cases where such issues are apparent to the pastoral counselor, a referral to a qualified psychological provider is the course taken, a practice consistent with the Code of Ethics of the American Association of Pastoral Counselors (AAPC, 1994). The AAPC organization has a membership over 3,000 across the nation (AAPC, 1994) with members from church-based, clinic-based, military-based, and school-based settings.

Spiritually Oriented Psychotherapy

Larry Crabb (1975, 1977, 1993, 1997, 2001) has been an outspoken leader in the field of Christian counseling and spiritually oriented psychotherapy over the past 30 years. His contribution to the discipline through his books and lectures has been of considerable influence to spiritual practitioners. Crabb (1977, 1997) emphasizes the theological truth that Christians are endowed with a new heart at conversion that awakens in them a new appetite for God that overwhelms all other passions in life. McMinn (1996) states that "three essential categories...must be considered simultaneously: psychology, theology, and spirituality" (pp.269-270).

Treatment approaches cover a wide range of secular and spiritual theories (Benner, 2002; Karasu, 1999; Shafranske, 1996). Much like the psychological provider in the secular context, the spiritual psychotherapist selects a treatment modality and intervention based on the presenting problem and need. Spiritual practices range from prayer to involvement of support from pastors and chaplains (Sperry, 2003). It is not certain how many of the 500,000 practicing psychotherapists in the U.S. are operating from a spiritually-based model, but quite likely that the percentage is significant and growing, based on a membership in the American Association of Christian Counselors (AACC) over 100,000 (Clinton, 2004).

One of the apparent distinctives of spiritually oriented psychotherapists is the choice of brief therapy strategies over long-term models (Kollar, 1997; Oliver, Hasz, & Richburg, 1997). The Christian community tends to associate long-term treatment with the psychoanalytic models of psychology and coils at the underlying premises and assumptions (Oliver et al., 1997). This phobic attitude, coupled with the prevailing call for increased accountability in the field from managed care enterprises and the general population may add to the attraction of these models. A theme in the current literature on spiritual psychotherapy is the necessity of maintaining a close link with the church on the part of practitioners in the field (Clinton et al., 2002). This subservient posture in relationship to the role of the church is a key characteristic of many Christian therapists, particularly those in the Protestant Evangelical community.

Clinton and Ohlschlager (2002) identify 10 tasks of the "competent Christian counselor" (p. 69), including:

intake/assessment, case formulation/treatment planning, individual counseling, marriage/family interventions, group counseling/discipling, spiritual direction, case evaluation/management, supervision/case consultation, networking/referral, and research translation/technology application (Clinton et al., 2002). The body of knowledge from this professional community is steadily growing and demonstrates an increasing effort to meet the earlier challenges in the field for reliable research in support of the spiritually-oriented theories and models (Clinton, 2004; Karasu, 1999; Koenig & Larson, 2001; Koenig, McCullough et al., 2001).

Implicit and Explicit Integration

It should be understood that not all spiritually-oriented psychotherapists adopt the same style or approach in their clinical work. The actual use of religion in clinical practice covers a continuum from implicit to explicit integration, the former being a more subdued approach in which the counselor embraces a worldview that is Christian-based, but not overtly discussed in the treatment context. Explicit integrationist, on the other hand, will adopt a very overt approach that might involve prayer, Scripture reading, and other spiritual practices for the benefit of problem resolution (Shafranske, 1996).

The current trend in the culture toward spirituality and religion poses challenging opportunities for mental health practitioners, regardless the worldview espoused (Stairs, 2000; Stone,

1999). The integration of psychology and theology requires a careful balance if one is to avoid the assumption of one discipline over the other (Bland, 2003). Tan offers some insightful comments, "Religion in clinical practice is therefore a crucial area for psychologists to develop competence in, both from a professional or clinical point of view, as well as from an ethical perspective (as cited in Shafranske, 1996). With this brief review of the three prominent models for spiritually-oriented treatments as a foundation, a limited discussion of relevant ethical issues and concerns follows.

Ethical Issues and Concerns in Faith-Based Counseling and Research

Over a decade ago Younggren (1993) raised concern that introducing spirituality and religion in psychotherapy may challenge the accepted scientific foundation for psychological theory and treatment. His assumption is that religious therapists are more likely to commit an ethical violation of boundaries in therapy than secular therapists. Data is not available to support or challenge his opinion, but it does speak to the necessity of sound ethics for professional conduct (Tan, 1994).

The AACC (Clinton, 2004) has developed its own Code for ethical conduct of its members, along with the AAPC (1994), both of which, Beck (as cited in Sanders, 1997) found in his analysis, address issues of competence, confidentiality, exploitation, colleague relationships, and deception. Clinical issues specific to spirituality can become quite complicated, as in the case of prayer, the purpose of which might vary significantly (Carmody & Carmody, 1990). Magaletta and Brawer (1998) identify a tripartite model of prayer in psychotherapy, where prayer can be practiced by the client alone, the therapist alone, or as a shared activity in which they both participate. The complexity of the intervention is heightened by the various types of prayer found in religious literature, including colloquial, petitional, ritual, and meditative prayer (Poloma & Pendleton, 1991). The two general principles at issue in the matter of prayer have to do with a restriction of the client's freedom and practicing beyond the scope of the provider's competence.

Tan (2003) offers a review of the ethical guidelines for integrating spiritual direction into psychotherapy. While most of these are consistent with professional practice, some are worth noting. A primary guideline is the respect therapists must have for their clients' right to hold religious beliefs that might differ from theirs (Richards & Bergin, 1997). Religion is diverse in its manifestations and it cannot be assumed that all Christians share similar values, convictions, and practices. This diversity requires the therapist to move sensitively into arenas of spirituality so as not to impose his own preferences on the client or hinder the therapeutic rapport.

Another important ethical principle concerns the therapist's requirement to determine a client's comfort level with a particular spiritual intervention prior to its use in the session. The principle of informed consent (APA, 2002) requires the professional to convey treatment intentions in a language and manner that the client can understand and choose to give or deny consent. More frequent interventions are reported by Christian psychologists to include prayer, theological referencing or teaching, and the use of Scripture. Less frequent spiritually-oriented strategies are spiritual relaxation, the healing of traumatic memories through guided imagery that usually involves a visualization of Jesus Christ, forgiveness, and spiritual homework (Clinton et al., 2002; Magaletta et al., 1998; Richards & Potts, 1995).

Ethical violations are a concern in a discussion of theological and religious integration into psychotherapy that must be taken seriously, however, as with most dilemmas of this nature, the final answers are less definable than the guiding principles that govern the practitioner in working with clients. Richards et al. (1995) proposes that those who do not address spiritual perspectives may be in violation of APA (2002) principles around respect for human diversity. Evidence of bias and prejudice against those who do espouse a religious worldview also requires attention, particularly as spirituality and religion becomes more diverse and prevalent in society (Jones, 1994; Richards et al., 1995; Worthington, 1986, 1990). A mounting body of evidence supports the idea that the expectation of those in psychotherapy is that spiritual and religious issues will be addressed at some point (Sperry, 2003; Westfield, 2001).

Worthington, Kurusu, McCullough, and Sandage (1996) in their 10-year review on religion and psychotherapeutic processes and outcomes offer a strong encouragement for the professional community of psychotherapists:

> Religious experience is not only part of multiculturalism but also consistent with the overall direction of postmodern culture. The acceptance of some role of religion in counseling has thus exploded into the mainstream of counseling and clinical psychology over the last decade. (Worthington et al., 1996, p. 448)

Before concluding this work on integration, a look at some of the key research available in support of the model will now be explored.

Empirical Research in Support of Integration

Despite considerable empirical literature in support of a link between religion or spirituality and mental health (Koenig, 1998; Koenig et al., 2001; McCullough, Hoyt, Larson, Koenig, & Thoresen, 2000; Plante & Sherman, 2001), theoretically-driven empirical research explaining the relationship remains lacking (Hall, 2004; Hill & Pargament, 2003). Hall (2004) notes the "need to identify the mediating mechanisms underlying RS-mental health associations" (p. 67). Hall (2004) puts forth five central organizing principles integrating religion/spirituality with the basic principles of attachment theory, psychoanalytic theories, and multiple code theory. It is too early to tell how the field will respond to his paradigm and challenge. Certain biased assumptions have factored into this paucity of research, including the assumption that the construct of religion and spirituality is beyond scientific investigation, and the assumption that the subject does not lend itself to scholarly inquiry (Miller & Thoresen, 2003). The Society for the Scientific Study of Religion has published their quarterly Journal for the Scientific Study of Religion since 1961, building strong support for scholastic efforts in religious research (Miller et al., 2003).

Conceptualization and definition of the constructs poses a threat to research efforts in the field on the variables of religion and spirituality. When found in the literature, too often they have been incorporated as add-on variables without a central focus (Hill et al., 2003). Measures of religion and spirituality have appeared in the literature, lending greater credibility to the constructs and giving promise to future investigations (Bassett, Camplin, Humphrey, & Door, 1991; Ripley, Worthington, & Berry, 2 Koenig, McCullough et al. (2001) provided a systematic review of research on religion, mental health, social support and substance abuse in the 20th century (Koenig et al., 2001). Nearly 80% of the studies identified in the meta-analytic review found that religious beliefs consistently correlated to increased satisfaction in life, happiness, positive affect, and higher morale

(Koenig et al., 2001). The reviewers also located 101 studies exploring the relationship between religion and depression, two-thirds of which found decreased rates of mood disorders among the more religious of the participants (Propst, 1980; Propst, Ostrom, Watkins, Dean, & Mashburn, 1992). Propst et al. (1992) conducted a clinical trial comparing nonreligious cognitive-behavioral therapy, religious cognitive-behavioral therapy, pastoral counseling treatment, and a waiting-list of clients (n = 11). Other studies suggested decreased anxiety among the religiously active (Miller, Fletcher, & Kabat-Zinn, 1995; Razali, Hasanah, Aminah, & Subramaniam, 1998). The strongest outcome identified in the literature is the decreased likelihood for religious persons to abuse alcohol or take illicit drugs (Koenig et al., 2001).

Worthington et al. (1996) found that nonreligious and religious alike hold similar values about psychotherapy, but differ in their respective valuing of religion. Research on the role of religion in mental health has risen considerably over the past 20 years (Sperry, 2003; Tan, 2003; Worthington et al., 1996). In their 10-year review of the literature, Worthington et al. (1996) chose to delineate between religious and spiritual, using the former category in their study of journal articles between 1984 and 1994. Yet, even with this distinction, the investigators cite the necessity in the field for more research on the effect of integrating religious values and traditions in light of the growing plurality in the world. They conclude with an intriguing comment, "The world has changed dramatically, creating a different climate within which to see the role and future of research on religion and counseling" (Worthington et al., 1996).

Larson and Larson (2003) state that "spirituality/religion emerges in research as an often beneficial source of coping strength in helping in prevention, coping, and at times recovery from physical or emotional illness" (p. 37). In an exploration of the degree to which patients (n = 400) rely upon their religious and spiritual beliefs in dealing with mental illness, it was found that 80% relied upon religious beliefs and activities for coping, 65% found a reduction of symptom severity through such reliance, 48% found religion increasing in importance to them during the episode, and 30% went so far as to cite their religious beliefs and activities as the most important dimension of their wellbeing during the illness (Tepper, Rogers, Coleman, & Maloney, 2001).

Prayer as a Treatment Intervention

The use of prayer as a healing agent or activity is evident in a variety of life contexts, including the physical or medical when we or someone near to us is experiencing a life-distressing or life-threatening illness or crisis (Ai et al., 1998; Ai et al, 2002; Biggar, Forehand, Devine, Brody, Armistead, Morse, & Simon, 1999; Kennedy, 2002). Harold Koenig (2003), Associate Professor of Psychiatry and Medicine at Duke University Medical School and the Director at the Center for the Study of

Religion/Spirituality and Health at the Duke University Medical Center, has authored nearly 200 scientific articles and dozens of books and chapters on the role of prayer in medical settings. The results of one such study, a three-year research at Duke on intercessory prayer was reported at a meeting of the American College of Cardiology (Koenig, 2003). He comments on the study:

> This double-blinded study involved 750 heart patients from throughout the USA and 26 prayer groups from around the world, including Christians in Manchester, Buddhists in Nepal, and Sufi Muslims and Carmelite nuns in America. Half of the patients in the study were prayed for, but nobody involved in the study, nor the participants, knew which half. According to the British Broadcasting Corporation (BBC) news and a special on the Discovery Channel TV program, prayer made no significant difference in the long-term health of the patients studied. (Koenig, 2003, p. 26)

While these kind of outcomes can be discouraging in the field of inquiry on prayer, it is important to point out some of the inherent problems with any scientific study of prayer. The type of research undertaken by Koenig (2003) and others in the medical field is quite difficult for a number of reasons. First, from a methodological standpoint, prayer is very hard to control for in conducting research. Consider the challenge of restraining family members and friends from praying for an ailing loved one or friend. If the control group is not a pure one, the internal validity of the design is at risk (Bernard, 2000; Creswell, 2003). Chibnall, Jeral, and Cerullo (2001) brought light to the problems in identifying the effectiveness of prayer when they discovered that Catholic Christians have weekly prayers for all the sick, presumably establishing a background level of prayer for everyone. Further, the theological implications and expectations around prayer pose several problems, considering that some faith traditions would see physical healing of the body from a diseased condition as answer to intercessory prayer, while others might see death itself as an ultimate form of healing for the patient who is then able to enter into an eternal state of peace. The Duke study (Koenig, 2003) does not have to weaken confidence in prayer as an intervention in any context, whether medical or psychological, but it does raise relevant questions about how far research can go in lending credibility to any metaphysical outcomes from intercessory prayer.

A key distinctive of this present study is the methodology of the experimental design, involving married partners in praying for their spouses. As has been discussed previously, spousal sentiment is not a stable factor in marriage (Doherty, 1981a, 1981b; Fincham et al., 1987; Gottman & Notarius, 2000; Hawkins et al., 2002). This work does not so much aim to establish a scientific basis for the theological or metaphysical efficacy of prayer as an intervention for couples, although the author maintains a confidence in such, rather to determine how the recitation of marriage-oriented prayers by the partners affects the sentiment of the partners, as tested through the use of valdiated measures of marital satisfaction.

Prayer as a Cognitive Psychological Intervention

Given the elusive nature of prayer it is necessary to delineate how intercessory prayer is identified in this research as an intervention aimed to alter married partners' thoughts, feelings, and sentiments toward each other. Richard Foster (1992) offers the most useful way of distinguishing between the various types of prayers found in Christian circles. He contends that prayer essentially connects the one praying to some specific reality, using factor analytic terms, he advocates a general prayer factor out of which three specific types of prayer emerge, including inward, outward, and upward prayers (Foster, 1992). The focus of inward prayers is self-examination, while outward prayers are aimed at improving human-to-human relationships and upward prayers are focused on the human-divine relationship. In the present study outward prayers are the ones under examination, particularly as pertains to the spousal relationship. This kind of prayer considers no domain too small or insignificant to warrant attention in an effort to change some aspect of the relationship that is deficient, problematic, or in need of enhancement in some way. For this study the outward prayers are most relevant as pertains to marital issues and needs.

Cognitive theorists in the field of psychology have argued that apart from the theological and metaphysical properties or benefits of prayer, the activity of praying informs and influences cognition (Barrett, 2001; Lawson & McCauley, 1990). Thought processes of distressed married partners leaves them susceptible to increased negativity toward the spouse (Gottman, 1999; Jacobson & Gurman, 1995; Moller & Van Zyl, 1991; Montoya et al., 2004). This depleted cognitive mindset manifests itself in contemptuous expectations and attributions in the marital dynamic. Consider a wife in a distressed marriage where separation and divorce have been openly discussed, who now approaches her husband in an attempt to repair from the latest breakdown, only to have him respond with more withdrawal. Upon examination he reveals what he is thinking, "She just wants to look better in the eyes of the counselor next week. She's not serious about working things out. There's no way she'd apologize about anything!" Despite one partner's well-intentioned effort at reconciliation, the spouse is unable to respond cooperatively and the thought process of the latter factors heavily in the failure. He can no longer perceive his wife in a positive light, attributing the worst possible motivations to even considerate behaviors. This cognitive negativity frequently leads to a negative feedback loop with both partners sliding further into hopeless thinking and cascading toward divorce (Gottman, 1999).

The benefits of prayer for personal health are increasingly supported in the literature (Koenig, 1997; Koenig & Cohen,

2002; Larson, Swyers, & McCullough, 1998; Lauer, 2003). Observations from research suggest improvement in health and even life expectancy for those who are engaged in the activity of praying (Powell et al., 2003). Dossey (1993) views prayer as one of the best kept secrets in modern medicine. His work in the field of medicine on the health benefits of prayer have been heralded by a wide range of religious traditions. Despite criticism from his colleagues in the medical community he optimistically promotes prayer as an alternative medical treatment in the future of healthcare in the United States (Dossey, 1993).

It is unclear precisely how prayer works to promote physiological or psychological health in the life of the individual. The very act of contemplative introspection in the midst of a stressful lifestyle and culture may offer respite for the devout person given to consistent rituals of prayer. Some suggest it is the optimism and hope that comes from a foundation of faith behind the prayers offered (Ai et al., 1998, 2002). The present work builds on the premise that the recitation of prayers with relevant content to a particular life situation, in this case one's marriage and spouse, can effect a positive movement in the way that individual perceives the partner about and for whom he/she is praying. By altering that perception in a positive way, the prayers constitute an intervention targeted at the cognitive dimension of the two married partners (Barrett, 2001; Baucom et al., 1989, 1990, 1996; Beach et al., 1995; Hawkins et al., 2002).

Butler, Stout, and Gardner (2002) examined the use of prayer as a conflict resolution ritual in their study of religious couples and families (n = 217), building on an earlier study (Butler, Gardner, & Bird, 1998) that investigated religious' couples use of prayer to invoke God's involvement in marital process with a primary focus on conflict. The later study (Butler et al., 2002) used a mail survey, posing some concerns to internal validity of the design (Bernard, 2000), to gain responses to a Prayer-Conflict Questionnaire (Butler et al., 1998) from a sample of 53% Latter-day Saint, 28% Protestant, and 19% Catholic participants. The researchers reported:

> Religious couples reported statistically significant effects associated with their practice of prayer. Specifically, couples noted that prayer invoked phenomenological interaction with a meaningfully personified Deity (t = 26.64, p = .000). Characterization of their metaphysical experience with Deity as an interactional "relationship" (Butler & Harper, 1994) thus appears reasonable. Spouses' interactional experience included feeling emotionally validated (t = 14.22, p = .000). Spouses also noted that prayer increased feelings of mindfulness and accountability toward Deity (t = 30.05, p = .000). Prayer decreased negativity, contempt, and hostility (t = 19.81, p = .000), as well as emotional reactivity toward their partner (t = 27.88, p = .000). Associated with this experience of de-escalation were an increase in their relationship and partner orientation (t = 25.29, p = .000), increase of an

unbiased/systemic perspective and partner empathy ($t = 16.64$, $p = .000$), and an increase in self-change as compared to a partner-change focus ($t = 28.40$, $p = .000$). Finally, spouses reported an increased experience of couple responsibility for reconciliation and problem-solving in consequence of prayer ($t = 25.85$, $p = .000$), together with an experience of incremental coaching or help from Deity, as opposed to outright problem solving on their behalf ($t = 10.39$, $p = .000$). (Butler et al., 2002, p. 30).

This type of research holds promise for the present study, particularly the benefit for the participating couples in the domain of marital sentiment as indicated in the decreased negativity, contempt, and hostility, as well as the increase in partner empathy (Butler et al., 2002).

The implementation of prayer in psychotherapy has been recognized as a means for building therapeutic rapport with clients, inducing relaxation, establishing ritualistic structure within a family, and increasing client reflection (Denton, 1990; Loewenberg, 1988; Margaletta & Brawer, 1998). Ethical principles specific to prayer as an intervention in treatment, can be grouped into two categories. The first concern relates to the therapist's requirement to respect the freedom of the client in choosing to voluntarily participate in the treatment process (AACC, 2004; AAMFT, 2002; APA, 2002). This principle necessitates an awareness on the part of the clinician of his own biases and prejudices around religiosity and spiritual beliefs. The second principle at stake in the use of prayer as a treatment intervention with couples is the expertise and training required of the therapist with the intervention (AACC, 2004; AAMFT, 2002; APA, 2002). The practitioner's experience with prayer may be quite narrow, given the diversity in the culture regarding religious and spiritual beliefs and practice. This must be taken into consideration and caution should be exercised so as to discern properly whether this or any faith-based intervention is appropriate for the client(s). A thorough assessment of this aspect should be part of the comprehensive assessment undertaken by the therapist early in the treatment, facilitating the means to determine the potential efficacy and problems associated with utilizing such an intervention with the couple.

Types of Prayer and a Rationale for Scripted Prayers as a Marital Intervention

A decision to use prayer in marriage counseling opens the door to a more complicated decision about how to structure the prayers or, if using scripted prayers, which prayers should be used. Liturgical Christian traditions have relied heavily on the use of scripted prayers, often centuries-old (CCC, 1994; Foster, 1992). More contemporary traditions in Christianity are less prone to use written prayers, tending instead to pray spontaneously with free verse (Foster, 1992; Omartian & Hayford, 2003). Omartian (2000, 2004a, 2004b; Omartian et al., 2003), however, has found strong reception of her reliance on pre-written prayers among the contemporary, evangelical Christian community as evidenced by the sale of her numerous books on the subject, including such scripted prayers for couples, parents, and friends.

Asking couples to begin praying for their spouses is latent with problems of validity, without also assigning them the actual prayers to offer up for the partner (Bernard, 2000). Given the frequently distressed and deteriorated sentiment among married partners, the types of prayers they might recite are less inclined to affect the positive shift desired in their cognitive perceptions (Gottman et al., 2000; Hawkins et al., 2002; Jacobson et al., 2000; Ladd et al., 2002; Mahoney et al., 1999).

The face validity of the Omartian (2004a, 2004b) prayers reflects relevance for married couples as the author addresses a diverse number of marital issues. From basic attitude to finances, and even sexuality, Omartian (2004a, 2004b) includes prayers designed to bring the partners in the marriage relationship to pause as they reflect on their individual role in the marital interaction and their perceptions of the spouse. The popularity of her books is recognized by the noteworthy accomplishment of being on the top spots among Christian non-fiction paperbacks for over three years (Omartian, 2000).

Stormie Omartian is a popular writer, speaker, and author of eleven best selling books including *The Power of a Praying Wife*, which was in the top ten books for 50 consecutive months (Christian non-fiction paperback), including 37 months at number one. In May of 2002, the book broke a 21-year industry record by claiming the number one spot for 27 consecutive months. In September of 2002, her other books, *The Power of a Praying Woman*, *The Power of a Praying parent* and ***The Power of a Praying Husband,*** were numbers two, three, and four respectively under this book. The book was eventually replaced in the number one slot by her own book, ***The Power of a Praying Husband***, which was also a finalist for the Kip Jordon Christian Book of the Year Award for an unprecedented three years in a row. (Omartian, 2000, p. 1)

In addition to the subject relevance of the material in the Omartian (2004a, 2004b) prayer books, they are available in a bound format, which lends ease to their use by couples. The small size of the Prayer books (Omartian, 2004a, 2004b) permits them to fit in a purse, briefcase, or even a pocket. The spouses are able to keep the prayers readily at hand in their use during the period of intervention. While any prayer may be helpful in altering an individual's attitude and perspective, prayers that are written with typical marital issues, problems, and needs in mind have the greater potential for a positive outcome. Clinicians choosing to incorporate prayer as a treatment intervention will need to determine if the prayers chosen are appropriate for the types of presenting problems and conditions in the client couple.

Conclusion

Marital distress is a serious problem in this country with negative implications for vocation, health, children, and economics

(Amato et al., 2001; Rank et al., 1999; Ross et al., 1999; Stanton, 1997; Wallerstein, 2000, 2004). Despite efforts to improve in the field of marital treatment, outcome studies are not impressive, with a success rate between 30 and 35% (Gottman & Notarius, 2000; Jacobson et al., 2000). Although early preparation prior to marriage shows promise, the vast majority of couples will enter matrimony with little expectation of the problems they will encounter and minimal skills to address the condition (Markman & Hahlweg, 1993; Stanley, 1997, 2003; Stanley et al., 2001).

As the two partners in marriage respond to the daily challenges and stressors of life, they experience each other in new and less than enjoyable ways. The result is episodic negativity with fights and a growing distance in their marriage (Gottman, 1999; Markman, Stanley et al., 1994). With the distress of the marital breakdown, the partners find themselves feeling angry, hurt, and disappointed with each other. In addition, their thought patterns regarding the marriage and the marital partner take on themes of negativity and despair (Jacobson et al., 2000; Montoya et al., 2004). This cognitive and affective change represents a threat to the marital sentiment of the spouses that is both de-motivating and predictive of increased risk for divorce (Gottman, 1999; Hawkins et al., 2002).

People who participate in the religious activity of prayer on a regular basis often demonstrate attitudes of optimism that promote physical and emotional health (Ai et al., 1998, 2002; Chibnal et al., 2001; Dossey, 1993). In an attempt to affect a significant change on the cognitive attitudes of married partners, this study proposes to intervene by having the spouses recite two daily prayers on behalf of their counterpart in the marriage. The theory behind the intervention suggests that the prayers will alter the partner's perceptions of their respective contribution to the marital condition, as well as their views toward each other in the relationship. This alteration of perception will result in a subsequent change in their marital sentiment (Weiss, 1980). This positive change manifests itself in a felt experience of improvement in the marriage relationship. Their scores on the Dyadic Adjustment Scale (Spanier, 1976) before and after the experimental intervention of daily prayer will be used to determine their level of marital satisfaction for evaluation of effect.

As with any intervention in psychotherapy, the model will require testing and modification in order to find the right combination of prayers, format for reciting the prayers, and the optimum period of time for the intervention to produce the best results, however, this blend of cognitive research with religious/spiritual activity as a means to protect against marital distress and deterioration and even remediate against the same is promising.

CHAPTER THREE

Methodology Research Design

To what extent does 30 days of daily prayer by marriage partners result in a statistically significant improvement on marital satisfaction measured by the DAS dyadic adjustment scores? To what extent does 30 days of daily affirmation by marriage partners result in a statistically significant improvement on marital satisfaction measured by the DAS dyadic adjustment scores? And to what extent is the average change from baseline to follow-up significantly greater for the treatment-prayer group couples and the control-affirmation group couples? This study employed a quantitative design, specifically, a quasi-experimental nonrandomized control group pretest- posttest design with a convenience sample of Catholic and Protestant Christian married couples for both the treatment and the control group (Bernard, 2000; Creswell, 2003; Leedy & Ormrod, 2001).

In an evaluation of the effectiveness of spousal prayer as a marital intervention as compared to a spousal affirmations intervention for marital couples, this study is well suited to a quantitative design. Giving particular attention to the control of potential confounding variables in the experiment, a number of precautions are proposed, including the use of a treatment group with scripted prayers and a control group with scripted affirmations.

The selection of a quasi-experimental design was derived from the formidable obstacle of securing a true randomized sample for the work in light of financial and resource constraints. Utilizing a nonrandomized control group pretest-posttest design represents the most expedient approach yielded trustworthy results for the analysis and interpretation. A pretest allowed for an examination of the sample group means and standard deviations, which increased the likelihood of an inference of randomization among the two comparative groups.

All couples participating in the treatment and the control groups were tested at the beginning of the 30-day period with the Dyadic Adjustment Scale and again at the end of the period, at the conclusion of the interventions, whether the daily prayers or the daily affirmations. The couples' average dyadic adjustment scores on the DAS were used as the basis for analysis in the study.

Description of the Intervention and the Control Group

Treatment Group Intervention

The treatment group was administered an intervention consisting of the daily recitation of two spousal prayers (Omartian, 2004a; 2004b) over a 30-day period. The prayers are published in separate books for the husband and wife, adding to the ease of use for this intervention. The Omartian Prayer books (2004a; 2004b) were chosen for the intervention in this study for several reasons. In a study such as this one on prayer's effectiveness, was difficult to determine the kind of prayers that would be most effective to accomplish the desired end. After a thorough search for a series of prayers consistent with the theme of marriage and spousal attitudes, the Omartian material stood out as the most approximate choice. The author, Stormie Omartian, is a popular writer, speaker, and author of eleven best selling books, including *The Power of a Praying Wife*, which was the number one book in the Christian non-fiction paperback industry for 37 months and in the top ten books for 50 consecutive months (Christian non-fiction paperback). *The Power of a Praying Husband* was the number four book in this category for September, 2002 and eventually rose to the number one slot. This book was also a finalist for the Kip Jordon Christian Book of the Year

Award for an unprecedented three years in a row (Omartian, 2000). Given the face validity of the material's relevancy to the husband and wife relationship, as well as the popular reception of the books as evident from the sales and rating record, these were the optimum choice for this study on prayer and marital satisfaction.

Each day of the 30-day period, the married partners read a prayer in the morning and a prayer in the evening out of the Omartian (2004a; 2004b) books. The men used the book *The Power of a Praying Husband* and the women used the book *The Power of a Praying Wife*. These books each contain 60 prayers addressing subject matter pertinent to marriage, including spirituality, motherhood, fatherhood, emotions, sexuality, decision-making, and character. On day one of the 30-day period, the husband was to pray the following prayer from the book of prayers in the morning.

> Lord, create in *me* a clean heart and renew a right spirit within me (Psalm 51:10). Show me where my attitude and thoughts are not what You would have them to be, especially toward my wife. Convict me when I am being unforgiving. Help me to quickly let go of any anger, so that confusion will not have a place in my mind. If there is behavior in me that needs to change, enable me to make changes that last. Whatever You reveal to me, I will confess to You as sin. Make me a man after Your own heart. Enable me to be the head of my home and family just as You created me to be. (Omartian, 2004a, p. 8)

That same day, sometime in the evening, the husband was asked to pray the following prayer from the book of prayers.

Lord, show me how to really cover (wife's name) in prayer. Enable me to dwell with her with understanding and give honor to her so that my prayers will not be hindered (1 Peter 3:7). Renew our love for one another. Heal any wounds that have caused a rift between us. Give me patience, understanding, and compassion. Help me to be loving, tenderhearted, and courteous to her just as You ask me in Your Word (1 Peter 3:8). Enable me to love her the way that You do. (Omartian, 2004a, p. 10) Similarly, the women will recite two prayers each day during the 30-day period.

Although the prayers are not the same, they do speak to similar themes. On day one the women was to recite the following prayer in the morning.

Lord, help me to be a good wife. I fully realize that I don't have what it takes to be one without Your help. Take my selfishness, impatience, and irritability and turn them into kindness, long-suffering, and the willingness to bear all things. Take my old emotional habits, mindsets, automatic reactions, rude assumptions, and self-protectiveness, and make me patient, kind, good, faithful, gentle, and self-controlled. Take the hardness of my heart and break down the walls with Your battering ram of revelation. Give me a new heart and work in me Your love, peace, and joy (Galatians 5:22, 23). I am not able to rise above who I am at this moment. Only You can transform me. (Omartian, 2004b, p. 8)

That same day, sometime in the evening, the wife was asked to pray the following prayer from the book of prayers.

Lord, I confess the times I've been unloving, critical, angry, resentful, disrespectful, or unforgiving toward my husband. Help me to put aside any hurt, anger, or disappointment I feel and forgive him the way You do—totally and completely, no looking back. Make me a tool of reconciliation, peace, and healing, in this marriage. Make me my husband's helpmate, companion, champion, friend, and support. Help me to create a peaceful, restful, safe place for him to come home to. Teach me how to take care of myself and stay attractive to him. Grow me into a creative and confident woman who is rich in mind, soul, and spirit. Make me the kind of woman he can be proud to say is his wife. (Omartian, 2004b, p. 10)

Participating couples were given the option to pray the prayers in the book of prayers at a time of their choosing, providing they recited two each day over the 30-day period. It was not necessary for them to recite the prayers in the partner's presence, however, they were allowed to do so if they desired. To keep them on schedule they were each given a Prayer Tracking Log booklet (Appendix D) containing instructions, the pages of the prayers for each day for the 30- day period, and a place for them to record the date and check that they prayed the prayers on that day.

Oral instructions for reciting the prayers were given to the participating couples at Time 1 testing with the DAS. By using the Prayer Tracking Log with the Omartian (2004a, 2004b) Prayer books, the couples were provided clear guidance for their self-directed application of the prayers over the 30-day period.

Control Group Intervention

The use of a control group in this study permitted a more precise comparison between the proposed treatment intervention of prayer and a modified cognitive affirmation intervention found in the literature of marriage and family treatment (Gottman, 1999). Like the treatment group, the couples in the control group participated in a 30-day period of two daily recitations aimed at improving marital satisfaction as measured by the Dyadic Adjustment scores on the DAS.

The control group intervention consisted of a modified version of Gottman's (1999) 7 Week Course in Fondness and Admiration. Gottman's 7 Week Course is a series of statements for couples to think about that are designed to elevate their thoughts and sentiments toward each other in the marriage relationship. The Gottman (1999) intervention was modified slightly for this study to better parallel the Prayer-treatment intervention over a 30-day period. For example, on day one, the participating couples were to recite the thought, "I am genuinely fond of my partner" in the morning and again in the evening. On day two the thought was, "I can easily speak of the good times in our relationship."

Each couple in the control group received a booklet with two affirmations to be recited daily over the 30-day period. As with the treatment group, the participating couples received a Tracking Log (Appendix E) for increased validation in the design. Cognitive interventions of this nature are more common in individual treatment of mood disorders (Beck, Rush, Shaw & Emergy, 1979), particularly depression, however, the incorporation of such models within couples therapy is well documented in the literature (Baucom & Epstein, 1990; Baucom, Shoham, Mueser, Daiuto, & Stickle, 1998; Berger & Hannah, 1999; Christensen, Atkins, Berns, Wheeler, Baucom & Simpson, 2004).

Sampling

Twenty-eight (28) Catholic Christian couples and 20 Protestant Christian couples were solicited for the treatment group. Eighteen (18) Catholic and 20 Protestant Christian couples were also solicited for the control group. The sample population were solicited from the Indianapolis area through a written invitation in a publication by Family Counseling Associates (FCA) disseminated to clients, area Protestant and Catholic churches, and area businesses. Clients of FCA were not solicited by the clinical staff apart from the written literature that was made available in the waiting room of the professional offices. FCA is a private corporation established in 1993 as an outpatient mental health counseling center serving the greater Indianapolis area of Indiana with three office locations. The researcher is the founder and serves as the Executive Director of the organization, which has grown over the past 12 years to its current employment of 21 therapists representing a variety of mental health disciplines. The author also provides clinical services at FCA as a Licensed Marriage and Family Therapist (LMFT) under the Health Professions Bureau of Indiana. As a specialist in marital treatment, his interventions follow primarily an Integrated Couples Behavioral Therapy (ICBT) model.

Given the lack of funding for this current research study, the author relied on a convenience sample from the FCA outpatient practice, as well as those who may have read of the study in the organization's publication, *Integrity*. Although randomization would have added to the overall design of the study, pragmatism and limited resources required the use of a nonrandomized approach. This was given attention in the data analysis section of the work, possibly limiting generalizability to a degree.

Specifically, the invitation (Appendix A) for volunteers to participate in a study of affirmation interventions effect on marriage was inserted in the *Integrity Publication* of Family Counseling Associates (FCA), a quarterly newsletter distributed to local churches in the Indianapolis area, FCA's Employee Assistance Program (EAP) businesses of for their employees, FCA's

Membership Assistance Program (MAP) churches for their members, and the clients of the Family Counseling Associates counseling center 21 therapists. Interested couples from the churches, businesses, and FCA practice who read the invitation, and contacted the office of Family Counseling Associates (FCA) were advised by the FCA secretary of available days and times for the couple to come to the office location and receive the test, the instructions, and all the materials for the research study. In the initial phone contact, the secretary of FCA provided a basic overview of the research study and asked the couple if they were married, over 18 years of age, and Protestant or Catholic Christians.

If a couple currently in therapy at FCA expressed an interest in participating in the research study, the researcher referred them to the FCA secretary, also a member of the research team, to receive all the necessary materials, the informed consent form, cover letter, and instructions for the intervention. The couple's involvement in the research study was ancillary to their marital treatment and did not become a focus of the actual therapy. In the data analysis of the results, marital treatment was treated as a potential confounding variable around which statistical control was taken.

Assignment of inquiring couples to the treatment or control group was made based on three factors, including the religious preference of the couple, the number of participants needed for each group, and an attempt to maintain an equal proportion of

Catholic and Protestant couples in the control group. The design called for a minimum of 20 Catholic couples in the treatment group, 20 Protestant couples in the treatment group, 20 Catholic couples in the control group, and 20 Protestant couples in the control group. Assignment to the treatment group or control group alternated based on Catholic or Protestant religious affiliation in order to equally distribute the sample. For instance, the first Catholic couple responding to the advertisement invitation for the study was assigned to the treatment group. The second Catholic couple responding was assigned to the control group. The first Protestant couple responding to the invitation was assigned to the treatment group. The second Protestant couple responding to the invitation was assigned to the control group. This method continued throughout the solicitation period until the minimum number of 20 Catholics and 20 Protestants in each group was achieved for a period of 30-days. The researcher chose to continue adding couples to the groups, based on this random assignment, over the entire 30-day period, even if the number of couples participating exceeded the minimum of 20 Catholics and 20 Protestants in each group.

Both sample groups, treatment and control, were comprised of married couples espousing a Catholic or Protestant Christian belief system as demonstrated by an acknowledgement of the same on a demographic information form (Appendix C). All participating couples were 18 years of age or older, a married heterosexual couple, and Protestant or Catholic Christians. No other restrictions regarding marital duration, or characterizing distinctions were used to include or exclude participants in the sample. The requirements of heterosexual married couples, 18 years of age or older, acknowledging nominal identification with Christianity represented the minimal thresholds for involvement in this study of prayer and marital satisfaction.

Instrumentation (DAS)

This study used Spanier's (1976) Dyadic Adjustment Scale (DAS) to measure the level of marital satisfaction among the couple participants. The literature strongly supports that the DAS assesses an important construct utilized in explaining and predicting the characterization of marital relationships (Spanier, 2004). "More than 1000 scientific investigations have used the instrument, and many clinicians have found it extremely valuable in their practices" (Spanier, 2004, p. 1).

The Dyadic Adjustment Scale (DAS) is a 32-item rating instrument completed by either or both partners in a relationship. Each DAS item is rated with one of several responses. The response anchors vary somewhat, depending on the question. The DAS includes four subscales: a) Dyadic Cohesion; b) Dyadic Satisfaction; c) Dyadic Cohesion; and d) Affectional Expression. Each item is scored on only one subscale. A total adjustment score is calculated by summing the scores for the four subscales. Normative data are reported on a sample of 218 married couples and 94 divorced couples. Norms are presented separately for married and divorced couples. The DAS may be completed in about 5 to 10 minutes. (Spanier, 2004, p. 1)

The Dyadic Adjustment Scale (DAS) was designed by Graham B. Spanier, PhD, a professor at Pennsylvania University, "to enable couples to share their opinions on their relationship in a psychologically sound and structured way" (Spanier, 1998, p. 1). The Dyadic Adjustment score is a total scale score that provides an overview of the level of distress within a couple relationship. The Dyadic Consensus subscale assesses the extent of agreement between partners on matters important to the relationship, such as money, religion, recreation, friends, household tasks, and time spent together. The Dyadic Satisfaction subscale measures the overall amount of positive feeling in the relationship. Individuals who are satisfied with the relationship have few complaints about their relations and few doubts about the relationship's chances of success. The scale can be an indication of divorce potential, commitment to the relationship, and hope for the future of the relationship. The Affectional Expression subscale measures the individual's satisfaction with the expression of affection and sex in the relationship. The Dyadic Cohesion subscale assesses the common interests and activities shared by the couple.

The 6 point Likert scale used in the DAS ranges from "Always Agree" to "Always Disagree" for the first 15 items, "All The

Time" to "Never" for the next 7 items, "Every Day" to "Never" for the next item, "All Of Them" to "None Of Them" for the next, "Never" to "More Often" for the next 4 items, "Yes" or "No" for the next 2 items, "Extremely Unhappy" to "Perfect" for the next item, and a 6-item multiple choice selection for the final item on the scale.

The DAS is published by Multi-Health Systems (Spanier, 2004) and is available in a manual QuikScore form, as well as a computerized version. The QuikScore form automatically converts the raw scores to t-scores for the individual. The DAS can usually be completed in less than 10 minutes and scoring is relatively easy and fast. Among other clinical purposes, the DAS applications "include investigating the effectiveness of various treatment methods" (Spanier, 2004, p. 3).

The Dyadic Adjustment Scale is a frequently used and well-researched paper-and-pencil instrument for assessing relationship satisfaction (Cohen, 1985; Follette & Jacobson, 1985; Johnson & Greenberg, 1985). The manual reports "that the Dyadic Adjustment Scale is the most widely used assessment instrument for marital quality in the world" (Spanier, 2004, p. 1). Reliability studies by various experimenters demonstrate good internal consistency among items and stable scores over time for the total measure. Spanier (2004) reported a "total scale internal consistency reliability of .96" (p. 29).

Subscale internal consistency reliabilities range from .73 to .92 for Dyadic Consensus. The values of coefficient alpha range from .77 to .94 for Dyadic Satisfaction. The internal consistency coefficients Affectional Expression are somewhat lower, ranging from .58 to .73. Internal consistency reliabilities for Dyadic consensus range from .72 to .86. (Spanier, 2004, p. 29)

Three judges, not including Spanier himself, examined all items of the DAS for content validity, eliminating all unacceptable items about which they were unable to reach a consensus as to its meeting content validity criteria (Spanier, 2004).

Spanier (1976) administered the scale to 218 married persons and 94 divorced persons. Each of the 32 items in the scale correlated significantly with the external criterion of marital status. In other words, for each item, t tests revealed significant differences between the responses of the divorced sample and those of the married sample ($p<.001$). In addition, the mean total scale scores for the married and divorced samples were 114.8 and 70.7, respectively. These total scores are significantly different at the .001 level. (p. 31)

Strong evidence supports confidence in the DAS as predictive of important indices (Markowski & Greenwood, 1984; Meredith, Abbott, & Adams, 1986; Smolen, Spiegel, and Martin, 1986; Dobson, 1987; Kunzer, 1987; Handlers, 1984; Ting-Tommey, 1983).

Although the DAS provides for the conversion of the raw scores to t scores, the analysis used the raw scores of the participants given that the instrument employs a Leikert response scale to its 32 questions, making the data categorical, rather than continuous and to gain a more precise set of data on the participants' satisfaction ratings without the weakened conversion process.

The study used the manual, rather than computerized, form of the instrument. Scoring was completed manually as well, to reduce the costs involved in the research and minimize potential obstacles for participation that a computerized version of the instrument could pose to some participating couples.

A number of investigations have been conducted to examine the extent of agreement on spousal DAS scores, including a sample of 108 married couples (Antil and Cotton, 1982), reporting a cross-spouse correlation of .59 on the total Dyadic Adjustment Scale score. The temporal stability of the DAS is demonstrated in several studies. Stein, Girodo, and Dotzenroth (1982) reported 11-week test-retest correlations on the DAS of .96.

Support for the criterion-related validity of the Dyadic Adjustment Scale comes from a study of marital distress. Distressed and nondistressed couples have been identified by scores on the DAS (Gottman et al., 2002; Jacobson, Follette, & McDonald, 1982), making the DAS an ideal instrument for measuring the degree of change resulting from the proposed intervention in this study.

Data Collection Procedures

The couples volunteering to participate in the study were asked to come to the main office in Indianapolis to complete the Information Sheet (Appendix B), the DAS, receive their Prayer Tracking Journal with the Instructions (Appendix C) for the treatment group along with the Prayer book for husbands (Omartian, 2004a) and the Prayer book for wives (Omartian, 2004b), and the Thought for the Day Tracking Journal with the Instructions (Appendix D) for the control group and the daily thoughts (Gottman, 1999) for the 30-day period.

At the conclusion of the 30-day period, all couples were contacted to participate in the follow-up testing of the DAS in the same manner as the baseline testing, and the control group participants were offered the treatment intervention of the Omartian Prayers (2004a; 2004b). The couples were invited to meet with a research assistant at the FCA offices in Indianapolis where they were given the DAS and offered the alternative intervention with explanation. The choice to engage in the follow-up use of the treatment intervention involving the prayers was completely voluntary with no consequence for the couples who chose not to participate in the follow-up intervention.

Couples were asked to turn in their Tracking Journals for the interventions, however, the treatment group was permitted to keep the Omartian Prayer books (2004a; 2004b). As noted, the control group couples were also given the opportunity to receive a copy of the Omartian Prayer books for follow-up use to the Gottman intervention.

Data Analysis

All statistical analyses was performed using SPSS for Windows (SPSS 13.0). The study sample is described using measures of central tendency (mean and median) and dispersion (standard deviation and range) for continuous/ordinal scaled variables and frequency and percent for categorical scaled variables.

A correlational matrix, based on analysis of demographic data of the participating couples in both the treatment and control groups is included in the statistical results. If any of those factors was found to be statistically significant with the DAS scores, a factorial ANCOVA was considered as part of the analysis.

For hypotheses 1 and 2 one-tailed paired t tests were used to compare the DAS scores between baseline and follow-up. The average change in the test scores along with 95% confidence intervals is also reported. For hypothesis 3, the average change in DAS score from baseline to follow-up was compared between the prayer-treatment and affirmation-control groups using a two-sample t test.

The baseline DAS score was also compared between Protestants and Catholics using a two-tailed two-sample t test. If there had been a statistically significant difference between the two groups, then a repeated measures analysis of variance would have been performed to compare the change in DAS from pre to post between three groups, Protestant/Prayer versus Catholic/Prayer versus non-prayer. Because the level of difference did not reach a statistically significant threshold, the repeated measures analysis of variance was not necessary.

Throughout all of the statistical analyses, sensitivity was given to the assumptions for the statistical procedure being used (e.g. normal distributions). Where necessary, non-parametric techniques were used or variables were transformed to achieve normal distributions.

CHAPTER FOUR

Data Collection and Analysis

Frequency Tables/Bar Charts for Categorical Variables

Demographic information was obtained as part of the assessment. Participating couples reported their age, employment status, hours worked, years of education, religious preference, and whether they are in therapy. Averages for the couples were used for age, hours worked, and years of education. Frequency tables and bar charts are provided for all categorical variables.

Given that the question of whether the spousal prayer could have a greater effect on couples who espouse a Catholic or a Protestant religious preference, an attempt was made to equalize the sample between the two groups by using volunteers from respective churches responding to the bulletin invitation. With a breakdown of 53.5% Catholics and 46.5% Protestant, this has been satisfactorily accomplished. Table 1 shows the distribution of religious denomination of the couples who participated in the study. There were 46 Catholics, representing 54% of the total participating couples, and 40 Protestants, representing the remaining 46% of the couples.

TABLE 1. Frequency Table for Religious Preference

		Frequency	Percent	Valid Percent	Cumulative %
Valid	Catholic	46	53.5	53.5	53.5
	Protestant	40	46.5	46.5	100.0
	Total	86	100.0	100.0	

Protestant is a broad category that can include a wide variety of religious groups, including Baptist, Assembly of God, Independent Christian Church/Church of Christ, and a number of other religious denominations (Bock et al., 1988; Carmody et al., 1990; McDowell et al., 1983). No attempt was made in this work to further delineate between the Protestant affiliations, however, the distinction between Protestant and Catholic Christians is a more pronounced one, particularly with regard to the nature of prayer. Protestant prayer is usually recognized as more casual, personal and conversational in style, whereas Catholic prayer tends to be scripted, using written prayers with rich theological and historical meaning (Carmody et al., 1990; Foster, 1992; Gruner, 1985; Ladd et al, 2002; Lauer, 2003). Figure 1 is a bar chart which graphically depicts the Catholic/Protestant distribution of religious denomination among the sample group.

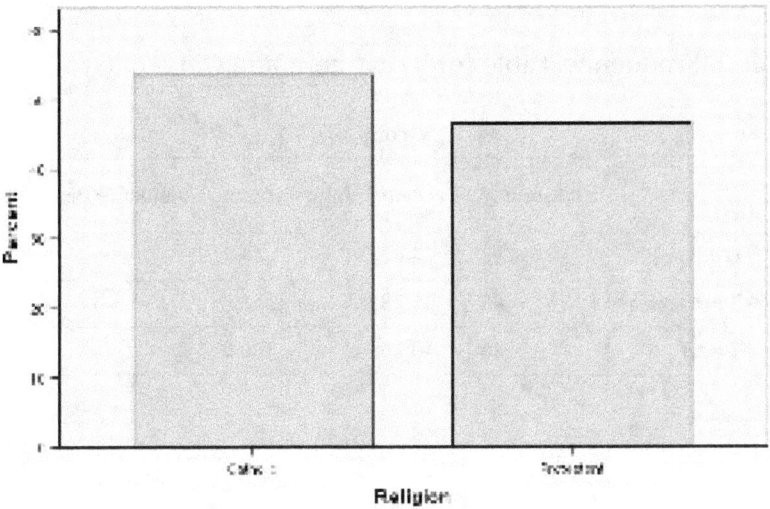

FIGURE 1. Bar chart for religious preference

The proposal called for a minimum of 20 couples in each of the four groups, including Catholic couples receiving the treatment, Protestant couples receiving the treatment, Catholic couples receiving the control intervention, and Protestant couples receiving the control intervention. In an effort to ensure a sufficient number for reliable results in the treatment group, additional couples were recruited for this group. The control group consisted of 38 couples, representing 44.2% of the total sample and the treatment group consisted of 48 couples, representing 55.8% of the total sample. Table 2 shows the distribution of the sample among the treatment and control groups. Figure 2 is a bar chart which graphically depicts the distribution of the sample into the two groups.

TABLE 2. Frequency Table for Treatment and Control Group

		Group			
		Frequency	Percent	Valid Percent	Cumulative Percent
Valid	Control	38	44.2	44.2	44.2
	Treatment	48	55.8	55.8	100.0
	Total	86	100.0	100.0	

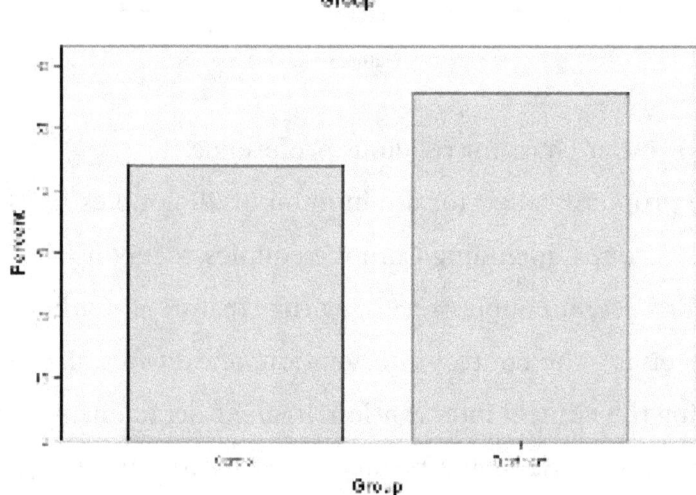

FIGURE 2. Bar chart for treatment and control group

Table 3 shows the distribution of Catholic and Protestant couples in the treatment group, a factor of significance in testing for a greater difference among the two groups. Figure 3 is a bar chart which graphically depicts the distribution.

TABLE 3. Frequency Table for Catholic and Protestant Couples in Treatment Group

		Frequency	Percent	Valid Percent	Cumulative %
Valid	Catholic Treatment	28	32.6	32.6	32.6
	Protestant Treatment	20	23.3	23.3	55.8
	Control	38	44.2	44.2	100.0
	Total	86	100.0	100.0	

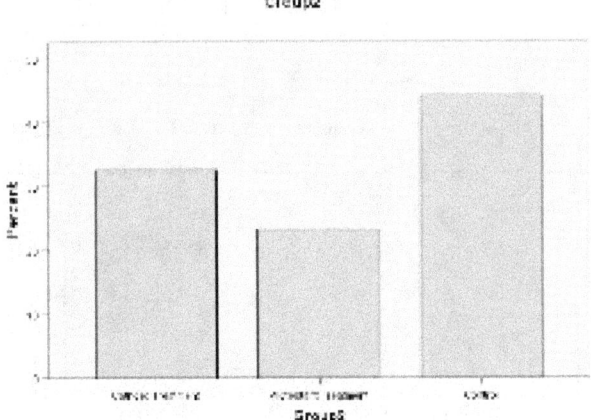

FIGURE 3. Bar chart for Catholic and Protestant couples in treatment group

Employment of the couples was given consideration as a variable possibly affecting baseline scores of the participants. Table 4 shows the distribution for couples according to employment. The majority of the couples, 53.5%, were both employed, 43% of the couples had only one partner employed, and 3.5% of the couples were neither employed. Figure 4 is a bar chart which graphically depicts the distribution.

TABLE 3. Frequency Table for Catholic and Protestant Couples in Treatment Group

		Frequency	Percent	Valid Percent	Cumulative Percent
Valid	Catholic Treatment	28	32.6	32.6	32.6
	Protestant Treatment	20	23.3	23.3	55.8
	Control	38	44.2	44.2	100.0
	Total	86	100.0	100.0	

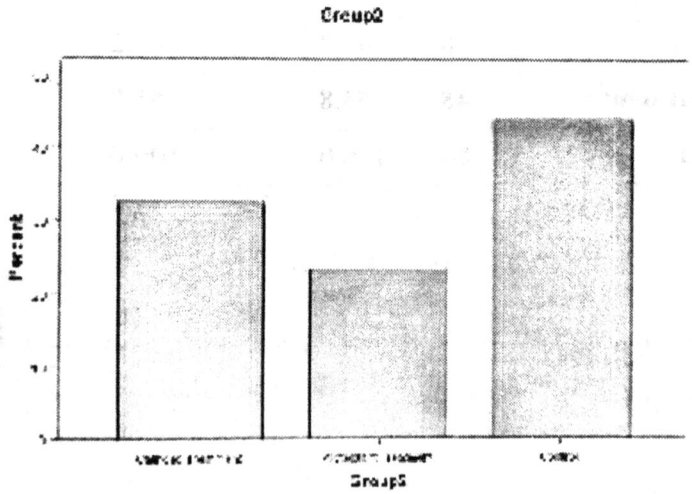

Figure 3. Bar chart for Catholic and Protestant couples in treatment group

Employment of the couples was given consideration as a variable possibly affecting baseline scores of the participants. Table 4 shows the distribution for couples according to employment. The majority of the couples 53.5% were both employed, 43% of the couples had only one partner employed, and 3.5% of the couples were neither employed. Figure 4 is a bar chart which graphically depicts the distribution.

TABLE 4. Frequency Table for Employment of Couples

		Frequency	Percent	Valid Percent	Cumulative %
	Neither employed	3	3.5	3.5	3.5
Valid	One employed	37	43.0	43.0	46.5
	Both employed	46	53.5	53.5	100.0
	Total	86	100.0	100.0	

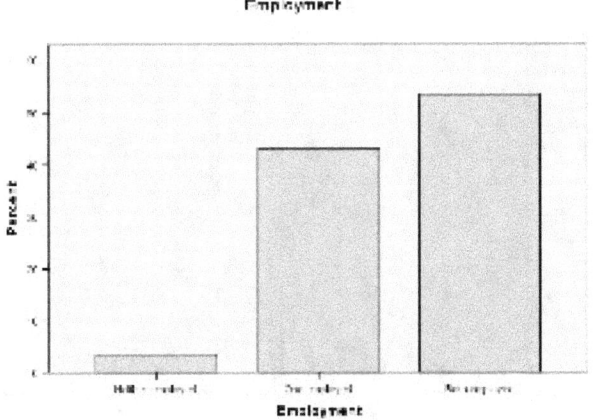

FIGURE 4. Bar chart for employment of couples

Finally, the couples volunteering for participation in the study were questioned as to whether they were currently receiving marital treatment. Table 5 illustrates that only 24.4% of the couples indicated they were in treatment, while 75.6% were not receiving treatment. Figure 5 is a bar chart which graphically depicts the distribution.

TABLE 5. Frequency Table for Couples Receiving Marital Treatment

		Frequency	Percent	Valid Percent	Cumulative %
				Tx	
Valid	Treatment	21	24.4	24.4	24.4
	No treatment	65	75.6	75.6	100.0
	Total	86	100.0	100.0	

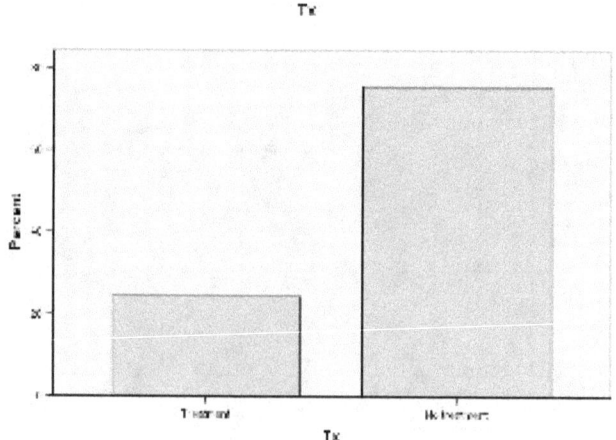

FIGURE 5. Bar chart for couples participating in marital treatment

Descriptive Statistics and Histograms for Continuous Scaled Variables

The following tables and histograms provide the statistical information in tables and histograms for all continuous scaled variables for the participating couples in the study. Table 6 shows that the average (*SD*) age for the couples was 41.9 (9.6) and the range was 28 to 77. Figure 6 is a histogram which graphically depicts the age distribution.

Table 6 shows that the average (*SD*) hours worked by the couples was 59.77 (22.232) and the range was 0 to 102. Figure 7 is a histogram which graphically depicts the hours worked distribution.

Table 6 shows the average (*SD*) scores for the couples at Time 1 baseline was 106.67 (16.557) and the range was 57 to 139. Figure 9 is a histogram which graphically depicts the baseline scores distribution.

Table 6 shows that the average (*SD*) scores for the couples at Time 2 was 113.337 (14.4270) and the range was 69 to 148. Figure 10 is a histogram which graphically depicts the Time 2 follow-up scores distribution.

TABLE 6. Statistics for Demographic Information

	Statistics						
	N		Mean	Median	Std. Deviation	Minimum	Maximum
	Valid	Missing					
Age	86	0	41.936	41.000	9.6023	27.5	76.5
Hours	86	0	59.77	60.00	22.232	0	102
Education	86	0	31.94	32.00	3.676	24	47
DA1	86	0	106.67	110.50	16.557	57	139
DA2	86	0	113.337	116.250	14.4270	68.5	147.5

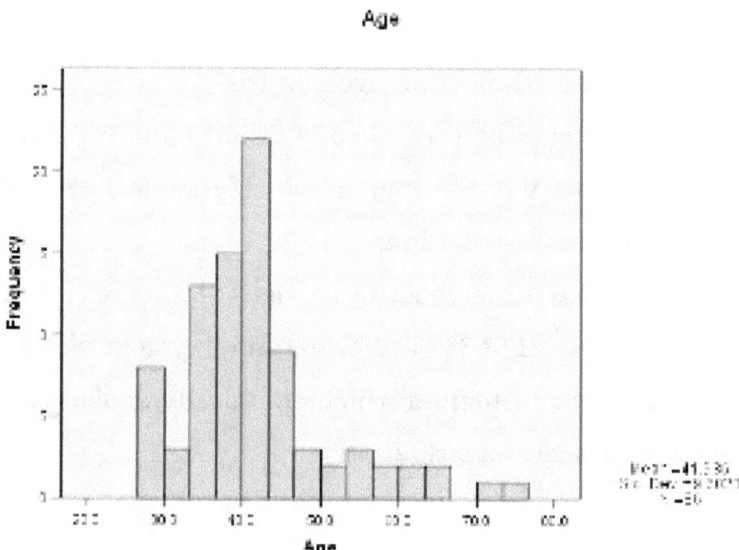

FIGURE 6. Age distribution

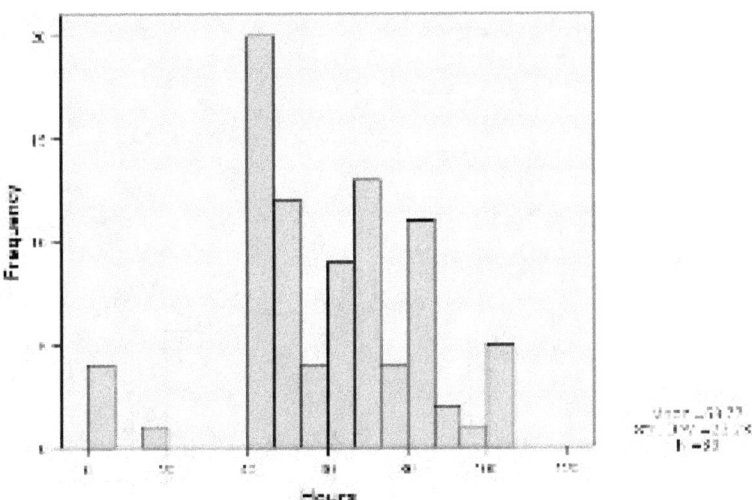
FIGURE 7. Hours worked

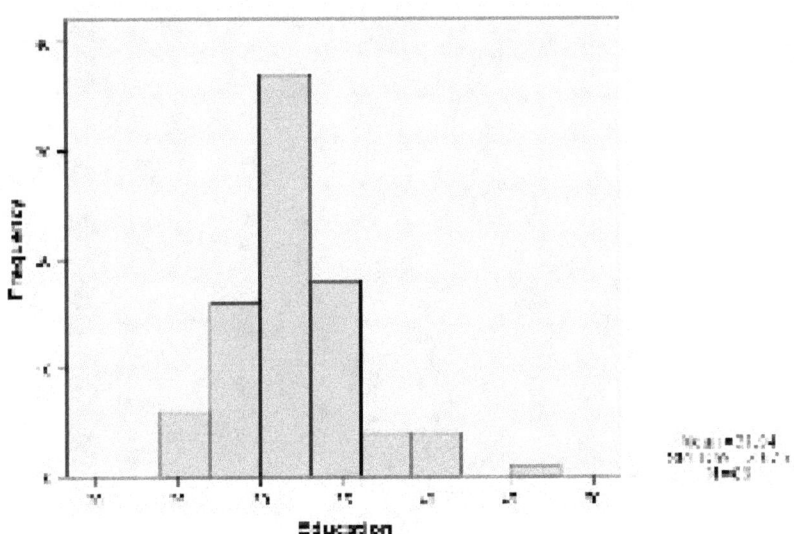
FIGURE 8. Education

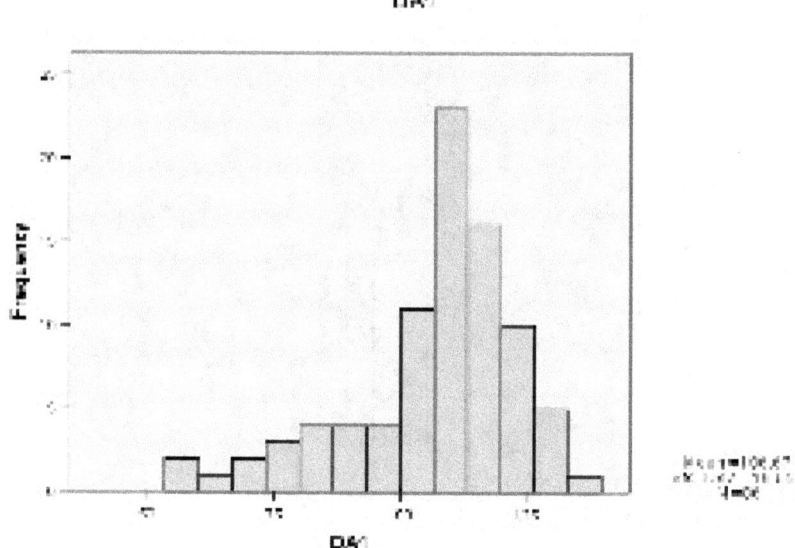

FIGURE 9. DAS scores at Time 1

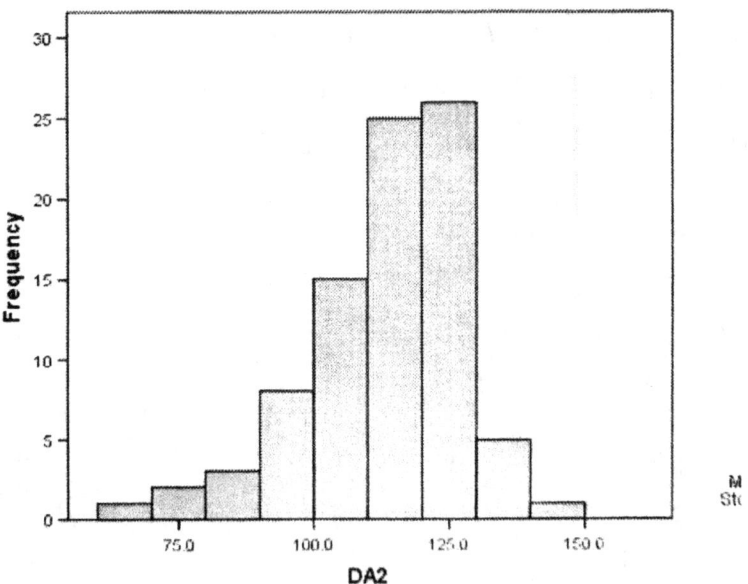

FIGURE 10. DAS scores at Time 2

Preliminary Analyses

Two-sample t test to answer the question: Is there a statistically significant difference in baseline DAS score between Catholics and Protestants?

The error bar chart which shows the average (and 95% confidence interval for the average) baseline DAS score, separately for the Catholic and Protestant groups. Along with Tables 7 and 8, these results show that the Catholic group had a statistically significantly larger baseline DAS score than the Protestant group. The average (*SD*) baseline DAS score was 111.3 (14.0) versus 101.4 (17.8) for the Catholic and Protestant groups respectively, *t*-2.87; *df*-84; *P*-0.005. The range for the Catholic group baseline DAS scores was 60 to 139. The range for the Protestant group baseline DAS scores was 57 to 128.

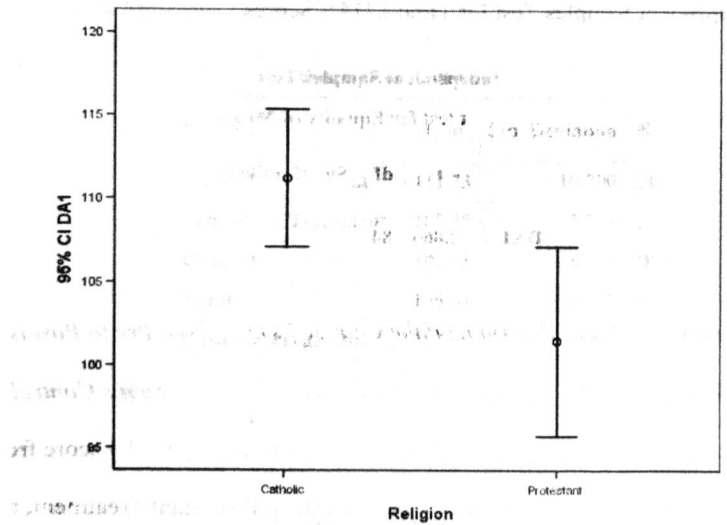

FIGURE 11. Baseline DAS scores for the Catholic and Protestant groups.

TABLE 7. Statistics for Time 1 DAS scores

	Religion	N Valid	N Missing	Mean	Median	Std. Deviation	Minimum	Maximum
DA1	Catholic	46	0	111.25	113.00	14.002	60	139
	Protestant	40	0	101.40	107.50	17.833	57	128

TABLE 8. Independent Samples Test for Time 1 DAS Scores

	t test for Equality of Means		
	t	df	Sig. (2-tailed)
DA1	2.866	84	.005

Repeated Measures ANOVA to Determine if the Change in DAS from Pre to Post is Different for the Three Groups, Catholic-Treatment versus Protestant-Treatment versus Control.

Figure 12 is a means plot which shows the change in average DAS score from pre to post, separately for each of the three groups, Catholic Treatment, Protestant Treatment, and Control. Along with tables 9 and 10, it is apparent that the change in DAS score from pre to post was not statistically significantly different for the three groups, F-1.19; df=(2, 83); P=0.31.

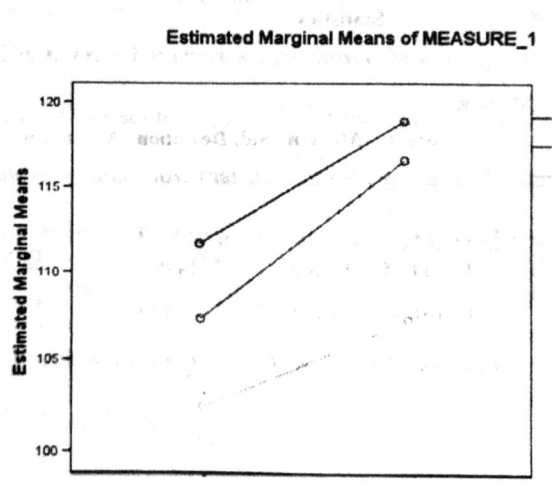

FIGURE 12. Estimated marginal means of Measure 1

TABLE 9. Descriptive Statistics

Descriptive Statistics

	Group2	Mean	Std. Deviation	N
DA1	Catholic Treatment	111.73	10.790	28
	Protestant Treatment	107.45	17.733	20
	Control	102.53	18.600	38
	Total	106.67	16.557	86
DA2	Catholic Treatment	118.893	10.9209	28
	Protestant Treatment	116.625	11.3750	20
	Control	107.513	16.1444	38
	Total	113.337	14.4270	86

TABLE 10. Tests of Within-Subjects Effects

Tests of Within-Subjects Effects
Measure: MEASURE_1

Source	Type III Sum of Squares	df	Mean Square	F	Sig.
Time * Group2	119.949	2.000	59.974	1.192	.309
Error(Time)	4175.704	83.000	50.310		

Pearson Correlation Analysis to Determine if Age is Associated with Baseline DAS Score

Figure 13 is a scatter plot which graphically depicts the relationship between age and baseline DAS score. Along with Table 11, it is apparent that there was not a statistically significant association between age and baseline DAS score, $r=0.066$; $P=0.55$.

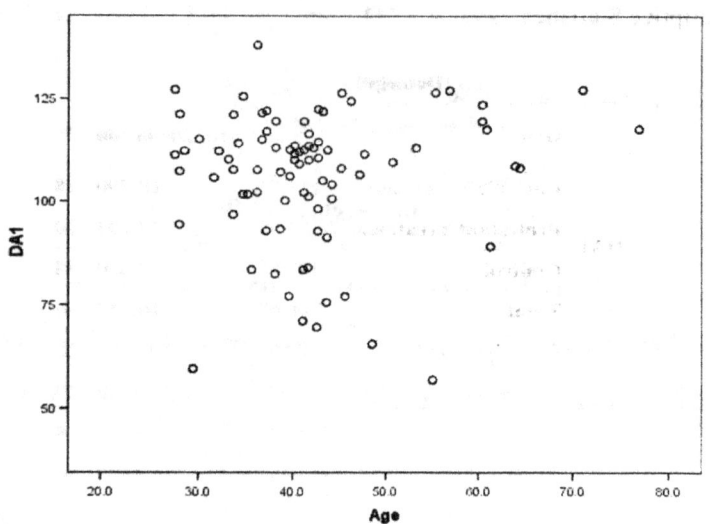

FIGURE 13. Scatter plot for age and baseline DAS score

TABLE 11. Age Correlations with Baseline DAS Score

Correlations		Age	DA1
Age	Pearson Correlation	1	.066
	Sig. (2-tailed)		.546
	N	86	86
DA1	Pearson Correlation	.066	1
	Sig. (2-tailed)	.546	
	N	86	86

Analysis of Variance (ANOVA) to Determine if Employment Status is Associated with Baseline DAS Score

Figure 14 and Tables 12 and 13 show that there was not a statistically significant association between employment status and baseline DAS score. The average (*SD*) baseline DAS score was 120.0 (10.1) versus 102.8 (17.3) versus 108.9 (15.7) for the "Neither husband nor wife employed", "Either husband or wife employed", and "Both husband and wife employed" groups respectively, $F=2.49$; $df=(2, 83)$; $P=0.089$.

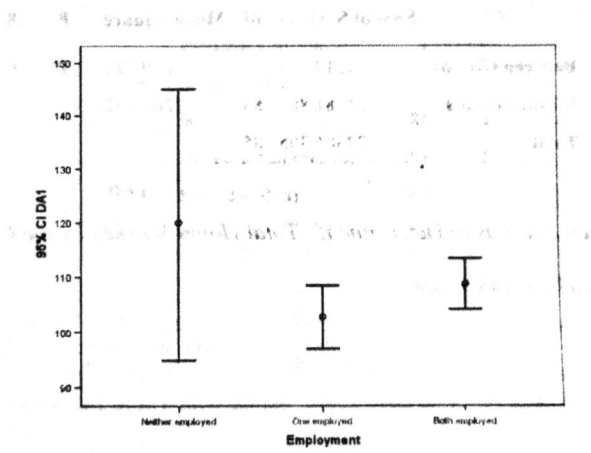

FIGURE 14. Histogram for employment status and baseline DAS score

TABLE 12. Employment Status and Baseline DAS Score

Statistics

		N		Mean	Median	Std. Deviation	Minimum	Maximum
	Employment	Valid	Missing					
DA1	Neither employed	3	0	120.00	124.00	10.112	109	128
	One employed	37	0	102.80	109.00	17.281	60	127
	Both employed	46	0	108.91	111.50	15.653	57	139

TABLE 13. ANOVA for Correlation of Employment Status and Baseline DAS Score

ANOVA
DA1

	Sum of Squares	df	Mean Square	F	Sig.
Between Groups	1319.423	2	659.712	2.491	.089
Within Groups	21981.882	83	264.842		
Total	23301.305	85			

Pearson Correlation Analysis to Determine if "Total Hours Worked by the Couple" is associated with Baseline DAS Score

Figure 15 is a scatter plot which graphically depicts the relationship between "total hours worked by the couple" and baseline DAS score. Along with Table 14, we see that there was not a statistically significant association between "total hours worked by the couple" and baseline DAS score, $r=-0.098$; $P=0.37$.

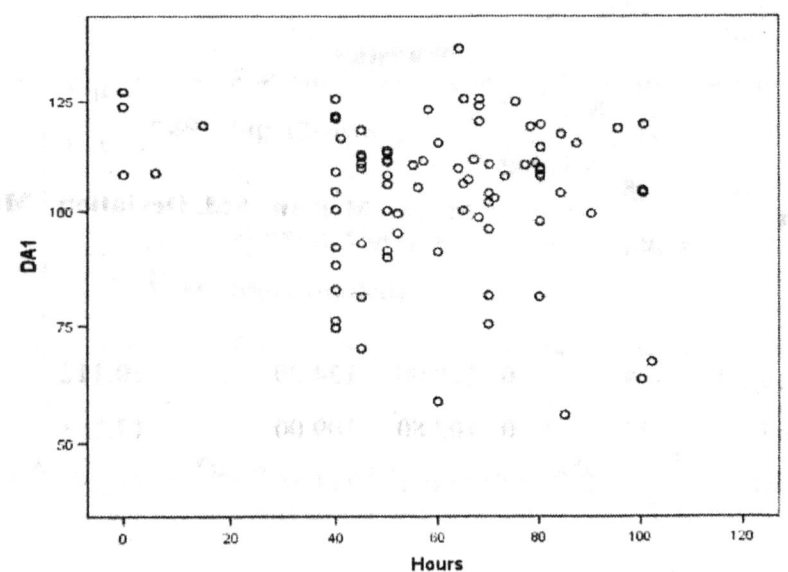

FIGURE 15. Scatter plot for Total Hours Worked and baseline DAS score

TABLE 14. Pearson Correlations for "Total Hours Worked" and Baseline DAS Score

		Correlations		
			Hours	DA1
Hours	Pearson Correlation		1	-.098
	Sig. (2-tailed)			.369
	N		86	86
DA1	Pearson Correlation		-.098	1
	Sig. (2-tailed)		.369	
	N		86	86

Pearson Correlation Analysis to Determine if "Total Years of Education for the Couple" is Associated with Baseline DAS Score

Figure 16 is a scatter plot which graphically depicts the relationship between "total years of education for the couple" and baseline DAS score. Along with Table 15, we see that there was not a statistically significant association between "total years of education for the couple" and baseline DAS score, $r=0.16$; $P=0.15$.

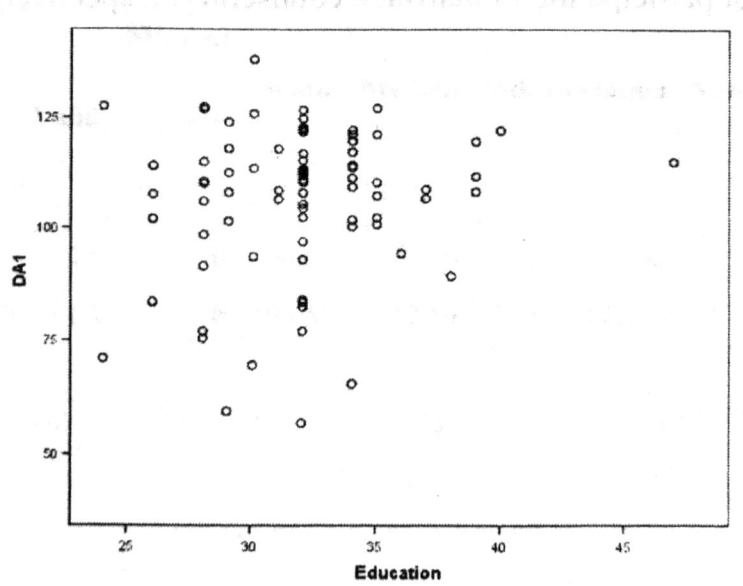

FIGURE 16. Scatter plot for total years of education for the couple and baseline DAS score

TABLE 15. Pearson Correlations Between Education and Baseline DAS Score

Correlations			Education	DA1
Education	Pearson Correlation		1	.155
	Sig. (2-tailed)			.153
	N		86	86
DA1	Pearson Correlation		.155	1
	Sig. (2-tailed)		.153	
	N		86	86

Two-Sample t test to Determine if Participation in Marriage Counseling (Tx) is Associated with Baseline DAS Score

Figure 17 and Tables 16 and 17 show that the group that were also participating in marriage counseling had a statistically significantly smaller baseline DAS score than the group that had no involvement in marriage counseling. The average (SD) baseline DAS score was 96.8 (19.1) versus 109.9 (14.4) for the group who were also participating in marriage counseling and the group who were not participating in marriage counseling, respectively, t=3.31; *df*=84; P=0.001.

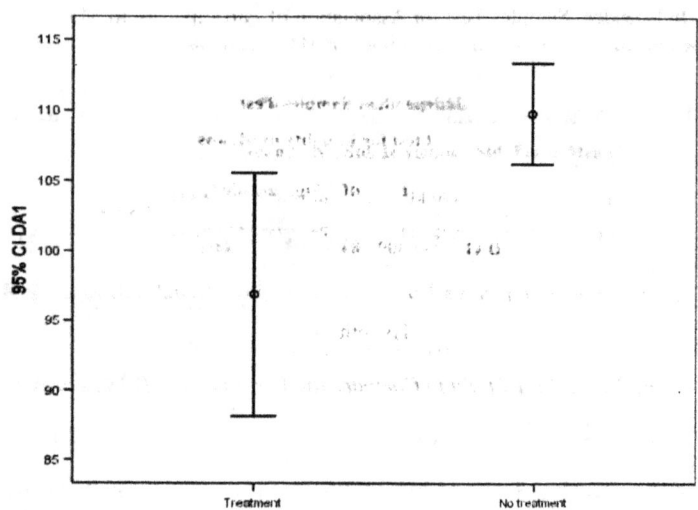

FIGURE 17. Association of marriage counseling and baseline DAS score

TABLE 16. Statistics for Participation in Treatment and Non-Participation in Treatment

	Tx	N Valid	N Missing	Mean	Median	Std. Deviation	Minimum	Maximum
DA1	Treatment	21	0	96.83	102.00	19.124	60	126
	No treatment	65	0	109.85	112.50	14.415	57	139

TABLE 17. Independent Samples Test for Association of Participation in Marriage Therapy with Baseline DAS Score

	Independent Samples Test		
	t test for Equality of Means		
	t	df	Sig. (2-tailed)
DA1	-3.309	84	.001

Hypotheses

Hypothesis 1: One-Tailed Paired t test to Compare the Pre and Post DAS Scores for the Treatment Group

Tables 18, 19 and 20 show that there was a statistically significant increase in DAS score from baseline to follow-up in the treatment group. The average (SD) DAS score was 110.0 (14.1) versus 117.9 (11.0) at baseline and follow-up respectively, t=-5.08; df=47; P<0.0001. Table 18 shows that the average difference (pre – post) in DAS score was -8.0 and the 95% confidence interval for the average difference was (-11.2, -4.8).

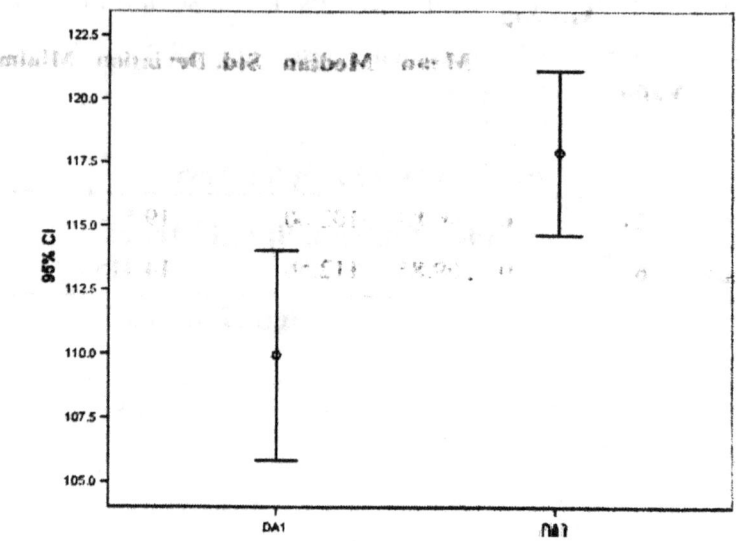

TABLE 18. Paired Samples Statistics of DAS 1 and DAS 2 for the Treatment Group

TABLE 18. Paired Samples Statistics of DAS 1 and DAS 2 for the Treatment Group

Paired Samples Statistics					
		Mean	N	Std. Deviation	Std. Error Mean
Pair 1	DA1	109.95	48	14.091	2.034
	DA2	117.948	48	11.0498	1.5949

TABLE 19. Results of the Paired Samples Test for the Treatment Group from Pre to Post

		t	df	Sig. (1-tailed)
Pair 1	DA1 - DA2	-5.078	47	.000

TABLE 20. Paired Differences for the Treatment Group from Pre to Post

		Mean	Std. Deviation	95% Confidence Interval of the Difference	
				Lower	Upper
Pair 1	DA1 - DA2	-8.0000	10.9146	-11.1693	-4.8307

Hypothesis 2: One-Tailed Paired t test to Compare the Pre and Post DAS Scores for the Control Group

Figure 19 and Tables 21, 22 and 23 show that there was a statistically significant increase in DAS score from baseline to follow-up in the control group. The average (SD) DAS score was 102.5 (18.6) versus 107.5 (16.1) at baseline and follow-up respectively, t=-3.5; df=37; P=0.0005. Table 21 shows that the average difference (pre – post) in DAS score was -5.0 and the 95% confidence interval for the average difference was (-7.8, -2.1).

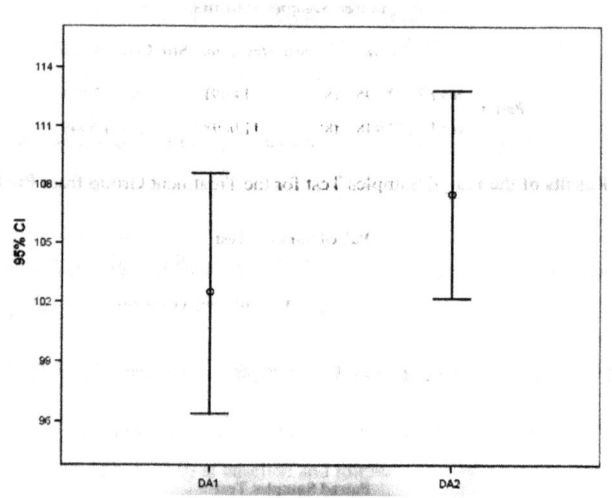

FIGURE 19. Comparison of the pre and post DAS scores for the control group

TABLE 21. Paired Samples Statistics for the Control Group

		Paired Samples Statistics			
		Mean	N	Std. Deviation	Std. Error Mean
Pair 1	DA1	102.53	38	18.600	3.017
	DA2	107.513	38	16.1444	2.6190

TABLE 22. Results of the Paired Samples Test for the Control Group from Pre to Post

		t	df	Sig. (1-tailed)
Pair 1	DA1 - DA2	-3.534	37	.0005

TABLE 23. Paired Differences for the Control Group from Pre to Post

		Paired Differences			95% Confidence Interval of the Difference	
		Mean	Std. Deviation	Std. Error Mean	Lower	Upper
Pair 1	DA1 - DA2	-4.9868	8.6988	1.4111	-7.8461	-2.1276

Hypothesis 3: Two-sample t test to Compare the Average Change in DAS from Baseline to Follow-up, Between the Treatment and Control Groups

Figure 20 and Tables 24 and 25 show that there was not a statistically significant difference in the average increase in DAS score from baseline to follow-up, between the treatment and control groups. The average (SD) increase in DAS score from baseline to follow-up was 5.0 (8.7) versus 8.0 (10.9) for the control and treatment groups respectively, t=-1.39, df=84, P=0.17.

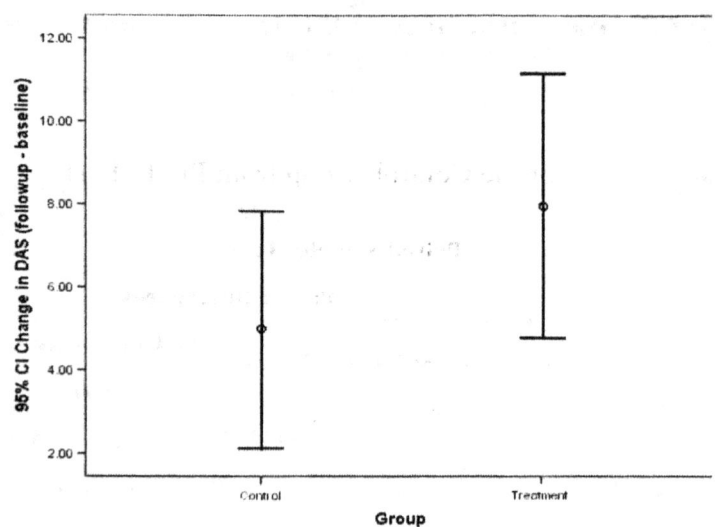

FIGURE 20. Comparison of the average change pre and post DAS scores for the treatment and control groups

TABLE 24. Statistics for Comparison of Average Change in DAS from Pre to Post Between Treatment and Control Groups

		Statistics						
		N						
	Group	Valid	Missing	Mean	Median	Std. Deviation	Minimum	Maximum
DA_Average Change in DAS (follow up - baseline)	Control	38	0	4.9868	5.0000	8.69878	-11.00	28.50
	Treatment	48	0	8.0000	6.5000	10.91456	-10.50	66.00

TABLE 25. Independent Samples Test Statistics for Comparison of Average Change in DAS from Pre to Post Between Treatment and Control Groups

		Statistics						
		N						
	Group	Valid	Missing	Mean	Median	Std. Deviation	Minimum	Maximum
DA_Average Change in DAS (follow up - baseline)	Control	38	0	4.9868	5.0000	8.69878	-11.00	28.50
	Treatment	48	0	8.0000	6.5000	10.91456	-10.50	66.00

Exploratory Analyses

Analysis of Covariance to Re-test Hypothesis 1 After Removing the Effect Due to Participation in Marriage Counseling

Figure 21 is a means plot which shows the change in average DAS score from Pre to post, after statistically adjusting for the association between participation in marriage counseling and the baseline DAS score for the treatment group. Along with Tables 26 and 27, we see that there was a statistically significant increase in DAS score from baseline to follow-up, even after adjusting for the association between participation in marriage counseling and the baseline DAS score. The adjusted average DAS score was 104.7 versus 114.6 at baseline and follow-up respectively, $F=6.2$; $df=(1, 46)$; $P=0.008$ (one-sided).

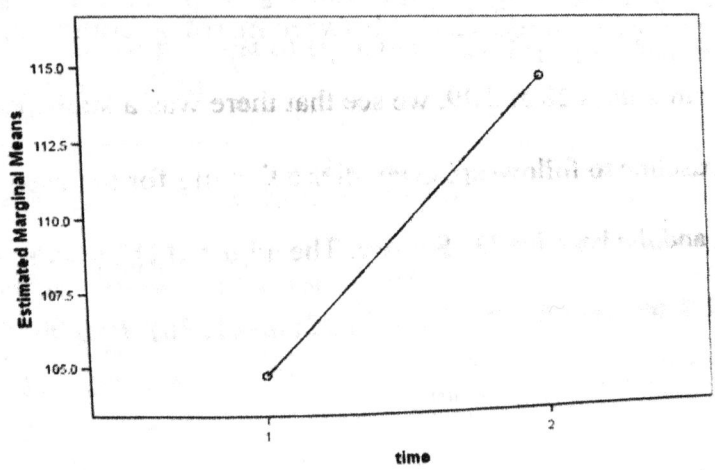

FIGURE 21. Means plot for change in average DAS score from pre to post of treatment group with control for participation in marriage counseling

TABLE 26. Tests of Within-Subjects Effects for Re-Test of Hypothesis 1 After Removing the Effect Due to Participation in Marriage Counseling

Tests of Within-Subjects Effects Measure: MEASURE_1					
Source	Type III Sum of Squares	df	Mean Square	F	Sig.
time	376.696	1.000	376.696	6.227	.008
Error(time)	2782.804	46.000	60.496		

TABLE 27. Statistical Results of Re-Test of Hypothesis 1 After Removing the Effect Due to Participation in Marriage Counseling

\multicolumn{5}{c}{1. time Measure: MEASURE_1}				
time	Mean	Std. Error	95% Confidence Interval	
			Lower Bound	Upper Bound
1	104.712	5.075	94.497	114.927
2	114.625	3.998	106.577	122.673

Analysis of Covariance to Re-test Hypothesis 2 After Removing the Effect Due to Participation in Marriage Counseling

Figure 22 is a means plot which shows the change in average DAS score from pre to post, after statistically adjusting for the association between marriage counseling and the baseline DAS score. Along with Tables 28 and 29, we see that there was a statistically significant increase in DAS score from baseline to follow-up, even after adjusting for the association between marriage counseling and the baseline DAS score. The adjusted DAS score was 102.5 versus 107.5 at baseline and follow-up respectively, $F=12.2$; $df=(1, 36)$; $P=0.0005$ (one-sided).

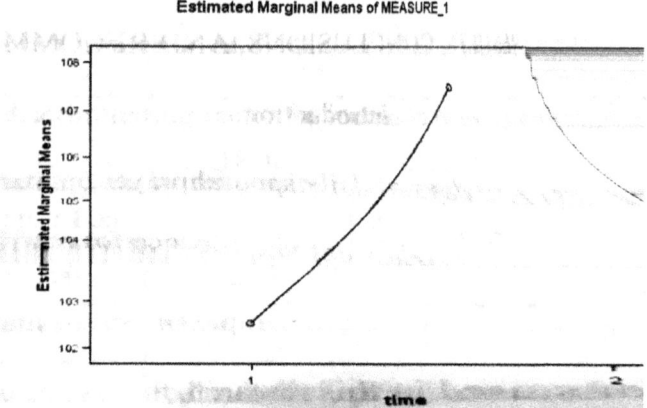

FIGURE 22. Means plot for change in average DAS score from pre to post of treatment group with control for participation in marriage counseling

TABLE 28. Tests of Within-Subjects Effects for Re-Test of Hypothesis 2 After Removing the Effect Due to Participation in Marriage Counseling

Tests of Within-Subjects Effects Measure: MEASURE_1					
Source	Type III Sum of Squares	df	Mean Square	F	Sig.
time	472.503	1.000	472.503	12.152	.0005
Error(time)	1399.789	36.000	38.883		

TABLE 29. Statistical Results of Re-Test of Hypothesis 2 After Removing the Effect Due to Participation in Marriage Counseling

1. time
Measure: MEASURE_1

time	Mean	Std. Error	95% Confidence Interval	
			Lower Bound	Upper Bound
1	102.526	2.895	96.654	108.399
2	107.513	2.469	102.505	112.521

CHAPTER FIVE

Results, Conclusions and Recommendations

This study on the effect of 30 days of daily spousal prayer on marital satisfaction has yielded results that have both clinical and practical significance for marriage and family practitioners and married couples. With a moderate sample ($n=86$) of married couples from both Catholic and Protestant denominations used in this research, the results can be more reliably trusted. What follows is an overview of the demographics of the sample, explanation of the results of the preliminary analyses, a thorough discussion regarding the research hypotheses in light of the results evident in the data, conclusions from the study, limitations in the work and recommendations for future research in the field of marital satisfaction.

Results of the Research

A number of variables were collected from the participating couples for consideration in the work, including age, employment status, hours worked, years of education, religious preference, and if they are participating in therapy at the present time. Because the couple is the unit under examination, as opposed to the individual, all data represents the average of the married partners.

Religious Preference

As has been explained earlier, the couples were recruited through an invitation that was published in church bulletins of both Catholic and Protestant Churches, and in the **Integrity Publication** of Family Counseling Associates. Conditions for participation in the research were minimal, including: the couple are married and they espouse a Catholic or Protestant Christian faith as indicated by their acknowledgement of the same on the Participant Information Form. No further exploration or examination of the faith or religious practice of the couples was taken into consideration as a discriminating factor for inclusion or exclusion in the study. The breakdown of couple participants by religiosity proved to be satisfactory, with 53.5% Catholic couples ($n=46$) and 46.5% Protestant couples ($n=40$). Of course, while Catholic Christianity represents a more unified and similar religious practice of worship and liturgy, Protestant Christianity is much more diversified in belief, practice and worship style, however, for the purposes of this study it was not deemed necessary to delineate the religious preference any further than this broad categorical representation.

In an attempt to equalize the treatment group and control group with the distribution of Catholic and Protestant couples, 28 Catholic and 20 Protestant couples received the treatment and 18 Catholic and 20 Protestant couples received the control intervention.

A two-sample t test was conducted to answer the question of whether a statistically significant difference could be found in the baseline DAS score between Catholic and Protestant couples. It was found that the Catholic group of married couples had a statistically significant larger baseline DAS score (mean=111.25) with a range from 60 to 139, than the Protestant group (mean=101.40) with a range from 57 to 128. It is unlikely that this finding is generalizable to the population at large and may be attributed to the fact that 14 of the 21 participating couples who were also receiving marriage counseling were Protestant, representing 67%. A reasonable assumption would be that the couple seeking or currently in marital therapy would be experiencing a level of relationship distress that would be identifiable on the DAS with a lower score. The explanation of involvement in marriage counseling addresses the question of why the Protestant couples' average score was lower than that of their Catholic counterpart.

A repeated measures ANOVA revealed no statistically significant differences between the Catholic Treatment, Protestant Treatment and Control groups for the change in DAS score from Time 1 to Time 2 at follow-up. The Protestant Treatment group experienced the greatest change in mean from Time 1 (107.45) to Time 2 (116.625). The Catholic Treatment group went from a mean of 111.73 at Time 1 to a mean of 118.893 at Time 2. The Control group mean at Time 1 was 102.53 and 107.513 at Time 2.

No conclusive findings are supported in the study to suggest that Catholics or Protestants will experience greater results from the spousal prayer treatment, however, the results do support a strong confidence in both the spousal prayer treatment and the control affirmation intervention in increasing a couple's marital satisfaction as measured by the DAS. This will be the topic of further discussion later in the paper.

Age

The average age of the couple participants was 42 (9.6023) with a range from 28 to 77. A Pearson Correlation analysis to determine if age is associated with baseline DAS scores revealed there was not a statistically significant association ($r=0.066$; $P=0.55$).

Employment

Employment of the partners was considered as a variable in the study, although the majority of the couples were both employed (53.5%). Couples with one partner employed represented the second largest group (43%) and the smallest group was the one where neither partner was employed (3.5%).

An analysis of variance (ANOVA) was conducted to determine if employment status is associated with the baseline DAS score of the couples in the study. There was no statistically significant association between employment status and the baseline DAS score. The lowest of the three groups was "Either husband or wife employed" with a score of 102.8 (17.3) and the highest of the three was "Neither husband nor wife employed" with a score of 120.0 (10.1). Since the statistical significance is not present in the data speculation for these results is not supported and it is doubtful we can generalize these trends among couples based on employment, particularly since the "Neither husband nor wife employed" group represented only 3.489% of the sample.

Hours Worked

The average number of total hours worked by the couples in the study was 59.77 (22.232) with a range from 0 to 102. A Pearson Correlation analysis to determine if "Total hours worked by the couple" is associated with the couple's baseline DAS score revealed there was not a statistically significant association between the two ($r=0.098$; $P=0.37$). Neither employment in itself or the number of hours worked can be cited in this study as accounting for the level of satisfaction in the couple's marriage at Time 1.

Education

The average number of years of education for the participating couples was 31.94 (3.676) with a range from 24 to 47. A total of 24 for the couple would indicate both partners completed high school. With a mean of 32 this sample reflects a higher-education group that may limit the applicability of the results to less educated populations. As with employment and total hours worked, a Pearson Correlation analysis was conducted to determine if "Total years of education for the couple" is associated with the baseline DAS score of the couple. As with the previous variables, a statistically significant association was not found in the data ($r=0.16$; $P=0.15$).

Marriage Counseling

Questioning regarding the couples' participation in marriage counseling found that 24.4% indicated they were in treatment. Given that a decision on the part of a couple to enter marital therapy is usually associated with a higher level of distress in the relationship and that therapy itself represents an intervention for positive change in the couple's marital satisfaction, it was important to control for this factor in order to determine statistical significance apart from the potentially confounding variable of involvement in therapy.

A two-sample t test was conducted to determine if participation in marriage counseling is associated with the baseline DAS score of the couples in the study. The average baseline DAS score of the couples in marriage counseling was 96.8 (19.1), as compared to the baseline DAS score of 109.9 (14.4) for the group who were not receiving marriage counseling, lower at a statistically significant level ($t=3.31$; $df=84$; $P=0.001$). The fact that the former couples in marriage counseling had lower scores on the baseline DAS supports the suggestion that a couple pursuing therapy are experiencing a lower level of satisfaction in their relationship.

An analysis of covariance (ANCOVA) to re-test hypothesis 1 with the treatment group after removing the effect due to participation in marriage counseling revealed that the increase in DAS score from baseline to follow-up was still statistically significant. The adjusted average DAS score was 104.7 at baseline and 114.6 at follow-up. As well, an analysis of covariance (ANCOVA) to re-test hypothesis 2 with the control group after removing the effect due to participation in marriage counseling also demonstrated a statistically significant increase in the DAS score from baseline to follow-up. The adjusted DAS score was 102.5 at baseline and 107.5 at follow-up for the control group.

This study has not attempted to associate the treatment intervention of spousal prayer with any other clinical intervention, only to determine the effect of the 30-day spousal prayer intervention on the couple's marital satisfaction level. Whether the prayers are given in the professional context by a marriage therapist or at the non-professional level, the effect is predictable.

Hypothesis 1

The first of the three research questions addressed in this study is whether 30 days of daily prayer by marriage partners results in a statistically significant improvement on marital satisfaction measured by the DAS dyadic adjustment scores. The first of the three statistical hypotheses is stated as follows:

H_0: The average DAS score is the same at baseline and follow-up for the treatment-Prayer group.

H_a: The average DAS score at follow-up is higher than the average DAS score at baseline for the treatment-Prayer group.

A one-tailed paired t test was performed on the data to compare the pre and post DAS scores for the treatment group who participated in the 30 days of daily spousal prayer. There was a statistically significant increase in DAS score from baseline to follow-up among these couples. The average (SD) DAS score was 109.95 (14.1) at baseline and 117.95 (11.0) at follow-up ($t=5.08$; $df=47$; $P<0.0001$). The average difference from pre to post in the DAS score was -8.0 and the 95% confidence interval for the average difference was (-11.2, -4.8).

With the results from this study, we can reject the null hypothesis for hypothesis 1 in support of the alternative hypothesis and conclude that 30 days of spousal daily prayer by marriage partners does result in a statistically significant improvement on marital satisfaction measured by the DAS dyadic adjustment scores.

Hypothesis 2

The second question addressed in this research is whether 30 days of daily affirmation by marriage partners results in a statistically significant improvement on marital satisfaction measured by the DAS dyadic adjustment score. The second of the three statistical hypotheses is stated as follows:

H_0: The average DAS score at follow-up is higher than the average DAS score at baseline for the affirmation-control group.

H_a: The average DAS score is the same at baseline and follow-up for the affirmation-control group.

To test the hypothesis a one-tailed paired t test was conducted to compare the pre and post DAS scores for the control group using the daily affirmations. The average (*SD*) DAS score was 102.15 (18.6) at baseline and 107.5 (16.1) at follow-up for the control group (t=-3.5; df=37; P=0.0005. The average difference between the pre and post DAS scores was -5.0 and the 95% confidence interval for the average difference was (-7.8, -2.1), revealing a statistically significant increase in the DAS score from baseline to follow-up.

The results of the data on the control group support the null hypothesis and are not sufficient to accept the alternative hypothesis. Thirty days of daily affirmation by marriage partners does result in a statistically significant improvement on marital satisfaction measured by the DAS dyadic adjustment scores.

Hypothesis 3

The third question in the research is whether the average change from baseline to follow-up for the treatment-prayer group is statistically significantly greater than the average change from baseline to follow-up for the control-affirmation group. The third of the three statistical hypotheses is stated as follows:

H_0: The average increase in DAS score from baseline to follow-up is the same for the prayer-treatment and affirmation-control groups.

H_a: The average increase in DAS score from baseline to follow-up for the prayer-treatment group is greater than the average increase in DAS score for the affirmation-control group.

To test hypothesis 3, a two-sample *t* test was conducted to compare the average change in DAS from baseline to follow-up between the treatment and control groups. There was not found a statistically significant difference in the average increase in DAS score from baseline to follow-up, between the two groups. The average (*SD*) increase in DAS score from baseline to follow-up was 5.0 (8.7) for the control group and 8.0 (10.9) for the treatment group (*t*=1.39, *df*=84, *P*=0.17).

As a result, the evidence from this study is insufficient to reject the third null hypothesis and accept the alternative. Although the average increase in DAS score from baseline to follow-up was greater for the treatment group than the control group, it did not reach a statistically significant level of difference and inferences will have to be limited in light of this result.

Limitations

Despite the strong evidence in support of daily spousal prayer and daily spousal affirmations over a 30-day period, this study is not without its limitations. Two pieces of demographic information about the couples, number of years married and whether this was a first or successive marriage, were omitted inadvertently, both of which would have been valuable in the analysis. Without that vital information, the application for couples at various stages of the marriage and family life cycle is uncertain, though still predictably beneficial. With that information we might well have been able to determine which couples, by years married, would most benefit from the prayer intervention. Whether the couple are in their first or a successive marriage may not be as critical as the years married, but it would have been intriguing to test for correlation with marital satisfaction as a factor in itself and also in combination with years married.

The sample for this research was drawn from predominately white middle to upper socio-economic class of married couples. While it is hoped that similar results could be expected with lower socio-economic populations and more diverse racial and ethnic groups of couples, this remains to be explored in future studies.

Given that 21 (24%) of the couples indicated they were also involved in marital treatment, we have no data about the type of therapy they are receiving and how the prayer intervention might better impact the overall effect of therapy when combined with traditional treatment.

The specific prayers (Omartian, 2004a; 2004b) chosen for this research, although selected for their applicability to typical marital issues and needs, as well as their scripted form for manualization, may also have limited application to certain styles of marriage and religious preferences. Utilization of other forms of prayer, or even individualized free-verse prayers by couples may have a different effect on the couples' marital satisfaction.

A final limitation that must be noted, though relevant to most research in the field of marriage and family studies, is the difficulty to control around potentially confounding variables. Although 30 days is not a long period of time, it is a sufficient amount of time for any number of experiences to take place that could impact a couple's level of satisfaction. As well, control for prayer is an even more difficult challenge in such research as this. Merely because the couples in the affirmation-control group were not administered the Omartian (2004a; 2004b) prayers does not ensure that those couples were not praying for each other over that same 30 day period. In fact, given that the couples were drawn from Catholic Churches, Protestant Churches and a faith-based professional counseling center, it is likely that the couples were engaged in some type and frequency of prayer for their marriage and possibly for their spouses in particular.

Conclusion

Essentially, this study has yielded support for the belief that 30 days of daily spousal prayer and that 30 days of daily spousal affirmations (Gottman, 1999) does make a statistically significant improvement in the marital satisfaction of couples as measured by the DAS dyadic adjustment score. What this study has failed to do is demonstrate that the 30 days of daily spousal prayer are more effective, at a statistically significant level, than an affirmation counterpart intervention of the same 30 day period.

In addition to this important result, the study has supported other studies that have found key demographic variables, such as age, employment, hours worked, and education do not correlate to marital satisfaction (Gottman, 1979; 1993a; 1994; 1996; 1999; Gottman et al., 2002; Markman, 1981; Markman et al., 1994).

Prayer is an effective intervention for married couples who are interested in improving their level of relationship satisfaction. More specifically, 30 days of daily spousal prayer does make a difference for the couple's marriage.

Recommendations for Future Research

This study has served as an introduction to research the association of faith-based interventions along with traditional cognitive therapy in order to impact marital satisfaction among couples. The particular interest of the researcher in prayer led to the choice of this religious practice, but the field of options for future research is limited only by the numerous and diverse practices inherent in the practice of religion and the methodologies available in the field of research to explore and examine the effect of these practices on marital satisfaction.

Case Study Follow-up

The moderate size of the sample used in this research study (n=86) has yielded valuable results to broaden our understanding of the potential effect of certain faith practices like prayer on a married couple's level of satisfaction, however, a case study methodology could add tremendous depth to the study, particularly if done as a follow-up to the present one. This might involve a case by case study of at least four couples, one from each of the representative groups examined in the work, including: a Catholic couple who participated in the prayer-treatment group, a Protestant couple who participated in the prayer-treatment group, a Catholic couple who participated in the affirmation-control group, and a Protestant couple who participated in the prayer-treatment group.

The interviews could include an exploration of the couple's religious practices, including corporate worship, personal devotion, and any other faith-building and faith-expressing activity. A better understanding of the above may assist the therapist, pastor, or other professional in designing and implementing a prayer intervention for marital improvement.

Isolate the Intervention Without a Parallel Control Intervention

The use of a control group was relevant to the design of this present study, however, it would also have been helpful to examine marital satisfaction stability over a 30-day period without any designed and intentional intervention. This could have been added to the design by testing the couples with the DAS at Time 1, re-testing at Time 2 after 30 days and administering the 30-day daily prayer-treatment, then re-testing at Time 3, 30 days later.

Use 60 Days for the Intervention

The Omartian (2004a; 2004b) prayers are convenient in their form as scripted prayers and their printed and published format in booklets, however, given that there are 60 prayers in the book series it might be expedient to draw the intervention period out over a 60 day period and instruct the couples to use just one prayer each day, rather than the two prayers prescribed in the treatment intervention for this study.

Other Faith-Based Interventions

The use of prayer as the treatment intervention, as noted previously, was based on the interest of the researcher to make application of a demonstrated intervention found beneficial in the medical realm to the psychological realm of marital studies. Yet, prayer is only one of many such faith-based interventions that could be administered. Asking couples to read a passage of Scripture from the Bible could be another way to offer a manualized form of intervention, particularly if the selected Scripture passages were drawn from texts relevant to marital themes. Asking a Catholic couple to attend daily Mass over a 30-day period would represent yet another faith practice that could yield significant positive results to the couple's satisfaction level. Engaging a Protestant couple in a weekly Bible study group that involved them in study and discussion with other married couples over a 30-day period could be considered a viable intervention.

The challenge is in somehow manualizing the intervention for consistency of effect and controlling for potentially confounding variables. With these recommendations in mind, future research in the field is limited only by the motivation and determination of the researcher.

Follow-up Testing for Longitudinal Stability of the Effect

One final suggestion for the current study is to conduct follow-up testing at some future date, likely 6 to 12 months, to assess for stability of the effect. As always, attrition of the sample will be a challenge for such follow-up attempts, but the results could greatly strengthen confidence in the intervention.

References

Ai, A. L., Dunkle, R. E., Peterson, C., & Bolling, S. F. (1998). The role of private prayer in psychological recovery among midlife and aged patients following cardiac surgery. **The Gerontologist, 38**(5), 591-601.

Ai, A. L., Peterson, C., Bolling, S. F., & Koenig, H. (2002). Private prayer and optimism in middle-aged and older patients awaiting cardiac surgery. **The Gerontologist, 42**(1), 70-81.

Alexander, F. G., & Selesnick, S. T. (1966). **The history of psychiatry: An evaluation of psychiatric thought and practice from prehistoric times to the present.** New York: New American Library.

Amato, P. R. (2000). The consequences of divorce for adults and children. **Journal of Marriage and the Family, 62**(4), 1269-1287.

Amato, P. R. (2001). Children of divorce in the 1990s: An update of the Amato and Keith (1991) meta-analysis. **Journal of Family Psychology, 15**(3), 355-370.

Amato, P. R., & Booth, A. (1997). *A generation at risk: Growing up in an era of family upheaval.* Cambridge, MA: Harvard University Press.

Amato, P. R., & Booth, A. (2001). Parental predivorce relations and offspring postdivorce well-being. *Journal of Marriage and Family, 63,* 197-212.

American Association of Christian Counselors. (n.d.). *AACC Mission.* Retrieved June 17, 2004, from http://aacc.net/

American Association for Marriage and Family Therapy. (2002). *Marriage, politics, and the AAMFT annual conference September, 2004.* Alexandria, VA: Author.

American Association of Pastoral Counselors. (1994). *Code of ethics.* Retrieved November 24, 2004, from http://aapc.org/ethics.htm

American Psychiatric Association. (1994). *Diagnostic and statistical manual of mental disorders* (4th ed.). Washington, DC: Author.

American Psychological Association. (2002, December). Ethical principles of psychologists and code of conduct. *American Psychologist, 57*(12), 1060-1073.

Anderson, N. T., Zuehlke, T. E., & Zuehlke, J. S. (2000). *Christ centered therapy.* Grand Rapids, MI: Zondervan.

Antill, J. K., & Cotton, S. (1982). Spanier's Dyadic Adjustment Scale: Some confirmatory analyses. *Australian Psychologist, 17,* 181-189.

Bakeman, R., & Gottman, J. M. (1986). *Observing interaction: An introduction to sequential analysis.* Cambridge, England: Cambridge University Press.

Bakeman, R., & Gottman, J. M. (1997). *Observing interaction: An introduction to sequential analysis* (2nd ed.). Cambridge, England: Cambridge University Press.

Barrett, J. L. (2001). How ordinary cognition informs petitionary prayer. *Journal of Cognition and Culture,1*(3), 259-269.

Bassett, R. L., Camplin, W., Humphrey, D., & Door, C. (1991). Measuring Christian maturity: A comparison of several scales. *Journal Psychology and Theology, 19,* 84-93.

Baucom, D. H., & Epstein, N. (1990). *Cognitive-behavioral marital therapy.* New York: Brunner/Mazel.

Baucom, D. H., Epstein, N., Daiuto, A. D., Carels, R. A., Rankin, L. A., & Burnett, C. K. (1996). Cognitions in marriage: The relationship between standards and attributions. *Journal of Family Psychology, 10*(2), 209-22.

Baucom, D. H., Epstein, N., Rankin, L. A., & Burnett, C. K. (1996). Assessing relationship standards: The inventory of specific relationship standards. *Journal of Family Psychology, 10*(1), 72-88.

Baucom, D. H., Epstein, N., Sayers, S., & Sher, T. G. (1989). The role of cognitions in marital relationships: Definitional, methodological, and conceptual issues. *Journal of Consulting and Clinical Psychology, 57*(1), 31-38.

Baucom, D. H., Shoham, V., Mueser, K. T., Daiuto, A. D., & Stickle, T. R. (1998). Empirically supported couple and family interventions for marital distress and adult mental health problems. *Journal of Consulting and Clinical Psychology, 66*(1), 53-88.

Beach, S. R. H., Etherton, J., & Whitaker, D. (1995). Cognitive accessibility and sentiment override—starting a Revolution:

Comment on Fincham et al. (1995). *Journal of Family Psychology, 9*(1), 19-23.

Beck, A. t. (1976). *Depression: Clinical, experimental, and theoretical aspects.* New York: Hoeber.

Beck, A. T., Rush, A. J., Shaw, B. F., & Emery, G. (1979). *Cognitive therapy of depression.* New York: Guilford Press.

Becker, G. S. (1991). *A treatise on the family.* Cambridge, MA: Harvard University Press.

Berger, R., & Hannah, M. (Eds.). (1999). *Handbook of preventive approaches in couple therapy.* New York: Brunner/Mazel.

Bernard, H. R. (2000). *Social research methods: Qualitative and quantitative approaches.* Thousand Oaks: Sage.

Bianchi, S. (1999). The gender gap in the economic well being of nonresident fathers and custodial mothers. *Demography, 36,* 195-203.

Biggar, H., Forehand, R., Devine, D., Brody, G., Armistead, L., Morse, E. et al. (1999). Women who are HIV infected: The role of religious activity in psychosocial adjustment. *AIDS Care, 11*(2), 195-199.

Birchler, G., Weiss, R., & Vincent, J. (1975). Multimethod analysis of social reinforcement exchange between martially distressed and nondistressed spouse and stranger dyads. *Journal of Personality and Social Psychology, 31,* 349-360.

Bland, E. D. (2003). Psychology-church collaboration: Finding a new level of mutual participation. *Journal of Psychology and Christianity, 22*(4), 290-303.

Blank, R. M. (1997). *It takes a nation: A new agenda for fighting poverty.* New York: Russell Sage Foundation.

Bloom, B., Asher, S., & White, S. (1978). Marital disruption as a stressor: A review and analysis. *Psychological Bulletin, 85,* 867-894.

Blummel, S. R. (1992). Explaining marital success and failure. In S. J. Bahr (Ed.), *Family research: A sixty year review, 1930-1990* (Vol. 2, pp. 1-114). New York: Lexington Books.

Bock, E. W., & Radelet, M. L. (1988). The marital integration of religious independents: A reevaluation of its significance. *Review of Religious Research, 29,* 228-241.

Brown, C. (Ed.). (1981). *The new international dictionary of new testament theology.* Grand Rapids, MI: Zondervan.

Bumpass, L. L., Martin, T. C., & Sweet, J. A. (1991). The impact of family background and early marital factors on marital disruption. *Journal of Family Issues, 12,* 22-42.

Burgess, E. W., & Cotrell, L. S. (1939). *Predicting success or failure in marriage.* New York: Prentice Hall.

Butler, M. H., Gardner, B. C., & Bird, M. H. (1998). Not just a time out: Change dynamics of prayer for religious couples in conflict situations. *Family Process, 37,* 451-475.

Butler, M. H., & Harper, J. M. (1994). The divine triangle: Deity in the marital system of religious couples. *Family Process, 33,* 277-286.

Butler, M. H., Stout, J. A., & Gardner, B. C. (2002). Prayer as a conflict resolution ritual: Clinical implications of religious couples' report of relationship softening, healing perspective, and change responsibility. *The American Journal of Family Therapy, 30,* 19-37.

Carmody, D. L., & Carmody, J. T. (1990). *Prayer in world religions.* Maryknoll, NY: Orbis Books.

Carrere, S., Buehlman, K., Gottman, J., Coan, J., & Ruckstuhl, L. (2000). Predicting marital stability and divorce in newlywed couples. *Journal of Family Psychology, 14,* 42-58.

Catechism of the Catholic Church (2nd ed.). (1994). Washington, D. C.: United States Catholic Conference.

Chamberlain, T. J., & Hall, C. A. (2000). *Realized religion.* Philadelphia: Templeton Foundation Press.

Cherlin, A. J., & Furstenberg, Jr., F. F. (1991). Longitudinal studies of effects of divorce on children in Great Britain and the United States. *Science, 252*(5011), 1386-89.

Chibnall, J. T., Jeral, J. M., & Cerullo, M. A. (2001). Experiments on distant intercessory prayer: God, science, and the lesson of Massah. *Archives of Internal Medicine, 161*, 2529-2536.

Christensen, A., Atkins, D. C., Berns, S., Wheeler, J., Baucom, D. H., & Simpson, L. E. (2004). Traditional versus integrative behavioral couple therapy for significantly and chronically distressed married couples. *Journal of Consulting and Clinical Psychology, 72*(2), 176-191.

Christensen, A., & Heavey, C. L. (1999). Interventions for couples. *Annual Review Psychology, 50,* 165-90.

Clinton, T. E. (2004). *American association of Christian counselors: About us.* Retrieved November 24, 2004, from http://aacc.net/

Clinton, T., & Ohlschlager, G. (2002). *Competent Christian counseling: Foundations & practice of compassionate soul care.* Colorado Springs, CO: WaterBrook Press.

Cohen, J. (1987). *Statistical power analysis for the behavioral sciences.* New York: Erlbaum.

Cohen, P. M. (1985). Locke Marital Adjustment Scale and the Dyadic Adjustment Scale. *American Journal of Family Therapy, 13,* 66-71.

Collins, G. R. (1998). *The soul search: A spiritual journey to authentic ministry with God.* Nashville, TN: Nelson.

Crabb, L. (1975). *Basic principles of biblical counseling.* Grand Rapids, MI: Zondervan.

Crabb, L. (1977). *Effective biblical counseling.* Grand Rapids, MI: Zondervan.

Crabb, L. (1993). *Finding God.* Grand Rapids, MI: Zondervan.

Crabb, L. (1997). *Connecting: Healing for ourselves and our relationships. A radical new vision.* Nashville, TN: Word.

Crabb, L. (2001). *Shattered dreams: God's unexpected pathway to joy.* Colorado Springs, CO: WaterBrook.

Creswell, J. W. (2003). *Research design: Qualitative, quantitative, and mixed methods approaches* (2nd ed.). Thousand Oaks, CA: Sage.

Denton, R. T. (1990). The religiously fundamentalist family: Training for assessment and treatment. *Journal of Social Work Education, 26,* 6-14.

Denver Seminary. (2004). *Academic programs.* Retrieved November 24, 2004, from Denver Seminary Site:http://denverseminary.com/catalog/index.php?page=38

deTurck, M. A., & Miller, G. R. (1986). Conceptualizing and measuring social cognition in marital communication: A validation study. *Journal of Applied Communication Research, 14*(2), 69-85.

deTurck, M. A., & Miller, G. R. (1986). The effects of husbands' and wives' social cognition on their marital adjustment, conjugal power, and self-esteem. *Journal of Marriage and the Family, 48,* 715-724.

Dobson, K. S. (1987). Marital and social adjustment in depressed and remitted married women. *Journal of Clinical Psychology, 43,* 261-265.

Doherty, W. J. (1981a). Cognitive processes in intimate conflict: I. Extending attribution theory. *American Journal of Family Therapy, 9,* 3-13.

Doherty, W. J. (1981b). Cognitive processes in intimate conflict: II. Efficacy and learned helplessness. *American Journal of Family Therapy, 9,* 35-44.

Dossey, L. (1993). *Healing words: The power of prayer and the practice of medicine.* San Francisco: Harper Collins.

Dudley, M. G., & Kosinski, F. A. (1990). Religiosity and marital satisfaction: A research note. *Review of Religious Research, 32,* 78-86.

Dunn, R. L., & Schwebel, A. I. (1995). Meta-analytic review of marital therapy outcome research. *Journal of Family Psychology, 9*, 58-68.

Edwards, T. (2001). *Spiritual director, spiritual companion: Guide to tending the soul.* New York: Paulist.

Ellis, A. (1962). *Reason and emotion in psychotherapy.* New York: Lyle Stuart.

Ellis, A. (1980). Psychotherapy and atheistic values: A response to A. E. Bergin's "Psychotherapy and religious values." *Journal of Consulting and Clinical Psychology, 48,* 635-639.

Ellis, A. (1988). Is religiosity pathological? *Free Inquiry, 18,* 27-32.

Fincham, F. D., Beach, S. R., & Baucom, D. H. (1987). Attribution processes in distressed and nondistressed couples: 4. self-partner attribution differences. *Journal of Personality and Social Psychology, 52*(4), 739-48.

Fincham, F. D., & Bradbury, T. N. (1989, November). *Cognition and marital dysfunction: The role of efficacy expectations.* Paper presented at the annual convention of the Association for Advancement of Behavior Therapy, Washington D. C.

Fincham, F. D., Garnier, P. C., Gano-Phillips, S., & Osborne, L. N. (1995). Preinteraction expectations, marital satisfaction, and accessibility: A new look at sentiment override. *Journal of Family Psychology, 9*(1), 3-14.

Follete, W. C., & Jacobson, N. S. (1985). Assessment and treatment of incompatible marital relationships. In W. Ickes (Ed.), *Compatible and Incompatible Relationships* (pp. 333-361). New York: Springer-Verlag.

Foster, R. J. (1992). *Prayer: Finding the heart's true home.* San Francisco: Harper Collins.

Fowers, B. J. (2000). *Beyond the myth of marital happiness.* San Francisco: Jossey-Bass.

Fowers, B. J., Montel, K. H., & Olson, D. H. (1996). Predicting marital success for premarital couple types based on PREPARE. *Journal of Marital and Family Therapy, 22,* 103-119.

Fraenkel, P., Markman, H., & Stanley, S. (1997). The prevention approach to relationship problems. *Sexual and Marital Therapy, 12*(3), 249-258.

Gallup, G. (1995). *The Gallup poll: Public opinion 1995.* Wilmington, DE: Scholarly Resources.

Geiss, S. K., & O'Leary, D. (1981). Therapist ratings of frequency and severity of marital problems: Implications for research. *Journal of Marital and Family Therapy, 7,* 515-20.

Gottman, J. M. (1979). *Marital interaction: Experimental investigations.* New York: Academic Press.

Gottman, J. M. (1993a). A theory of marital dissolution and stability. *Journal of Family Psychology, 7*(1), 57-75.

Gottman, J. M. (1993b). The roles of conflict engagement, escalation, and avoidance in marital interaction: A longitudinal view of five types of couples. *Journal of Consulting and Clinical Psychology, 61*(1), 6-15.

Gottman, J. M. (1994). *Why marriages succeed or fail: And how you can make yours last.* New York: Simon & Schuster.

Gottman, J. M. (Ed.). (1996). *What predicts divorce: The measures.* Hillsdale, NJ: Erlbaum.

Gottman, J. M. (1998). Psychology and the study of marital processes. *Annual Review of Psychology, 49,* 169-97.

Gottman, J.M. (1999). *The marriage clinic: A scientifically based marital therapy.* New York: Norton.

Gottman, J. M., Coan, J., Carrere, S., & Swanson, C. (1998). Predicting marital happiness and stability from newlywed interactions. *Journal of Marriage and Family, 60,* 5-22.

Gottman, J. M., & Krokoff, L. J. (1989). Marital interaction and satisfaction: A longitudinal view. *Journal of Consulting and Clinical Psychology, 57*(1), 47-52.

Gottman, J. M., & Levenson, R. W. (1992). Marital processes predictive of later dissolution: Behavior, physiology, and health. *Journal of Personality and Social Psychology, 63*(2), 221-233.

Gottman, J. M., & Levenson, R. W. (2002). A two-factor model for predicting when a couple will divorce: Exploratory analyses using 14-year longitudinal data. *Family Process, 41*(1), 83-96.

Gottman, J. M., Murray, J. D., Swanson, C. C., Tyson, R., & Swanson, K. (2002). *The mathematics of marriage: Dynamic nonlinear models.* London: The MIT Press.

Gottman, J. M., & Notarius, C. I. (2000). Decade review: Observing marital interaction. *Journal of Marriage and the Family, 62,* 927-47.

Greenstein, T. N. (2001). *Methods of family research.* Thousand Oaks, CA: Sage.

Griffin, E. (1994). *Clinging: The experience of prayer.* San Francisco: Harper & Row.

Gruner, L. (1985). The correlation of private, religious devotional practices and marital adjustment. *Journal of Comparative Family Studies, 16,* 47-59.

Hahlweg, K., & Jacobson, N. (Eds.). (1984). *Marital interaction.* New York: The Guilford Press.

Hahlweg, K., & Markman, H. J. (1988). Effectiveness of behavioral marital therapy: Empirical status of behavioral techniques in preventing and alleviating marital distress. *Journal of Consulting and Clinical Psychology, 56,* 440-447.

Hahlweg, K., Markman, H. J., Thurmaier, F., Engl, J., & Eckert, V. (1998). Prevention of marital distress: Results of a German prospective longitudinal study. *Journal of Family Psychology, 12*(4), 543-556.

Hahlweg, K., Revenstorf, D., & Schindler, L. (1984). Effects of behavioral marital therapy on couples' communication and problem-solving skills. *Journal of Consulting and Clinical Psychology, 52,* 553-66.

Halford, K. W., Sanders, M. R., & Behrens, B. C. (2001). Can skills training prevent relationship problems in at-risk couples? Four-Year effects of a behavioral relationship education program. *Journal of Family Psychology, 15,* 750-68.

Hall, T. W. (2004). Christian spirituality and mental health: A relationship spirituality paradigm for empirical research. *Journal of Psychology and Christianity, 23*(1), 66-81.

Handlers, S. L. (1984). Level of object relations and marital adjustment influencing parents' choice of childbirth procedure. *Birth Psychology Bulletin, 5,* 23-37.

Hawkins, M. W., Carrere, S., & Gottman, J. M. (2002). Marital sentiment override: Does it influence couples' perceptions? *Journal of Marriage and Family, 64,* 193-201.

Hetherington, E. M., & Kelly, J. (2002). *For better or for worse: Divorce reconsidered.* New York: Norton.

Helgeson, V. S. (1994). Relation of agency and communion to well-being: Evidence and potential explanations. *Psychological Bulletin, 116,* 412-28.

Henry, C. F. H. (1977). *God, revelation and authority.* Waco, TX: Word Books.

Hetherington, E. M., & Kelly, J. (2002). *For better or for worse: Divorce reconsidered.* New York: Norton.

Hill, P. C., & Pargament, K. I. (2003, January). Advances in the conceptualization and measurement of religion and spirituality: Implications for physical and mental health research. *American Psychologist, 58*(1), 64-74.

Howard, N. C., McMinn, M. R., Bissell, L. D., Faries, S. R., VanMeter, J. B. (2000). Spiritual directors and clinical psychologists: A comparison of mental health and spiritual values. *Journal of Psychology and Theology, 28*(4), 308-320.

Hu, Y., & Goldman, N. (1990). Mortality differentials by marital status: An international comparison. *Demography, 27*(2), 233-250.

Hunt, R., & King, M. (1978). Religiosity and marriage. *Journal for the Scientific Study of Religion, 17,* 399-406.

Institute for American Values. (2002). *Why marriage matters: Twenty-one conclusions from the social sciences.* New York: Author.

Jacobson, N. S., & Addis, M. E. (1993). Research on couples and couple therapy: What do we know? Where are we going? *Journal of Consulting and Clinical Psychology, 61*(1), 85-93.

Jacobson, N. S., Christensen, A., Prince, S. E., Cordova, J., & Eldridge, K. (2000). Integrative behavioral couple therapy: An acceptance-based, promising new treatment for couple discord. *Journal of Consulting and Clinical Psychology, 68*(2), 351-355.

Jacobson, N. S., Follette, W. C., & McDonald, D. W. (1982). Reactivity to positive and negative behavior in distressed and nondistressed married couples. *Journal of Consulting and Clinical Psychology, 50,* 706-714.

Jacobson, N. S. Gottman, J. M., Gortner, E., Berns, S., & Shortt, J. W. (1996). Psychological factors in the longitudinal course of battering: When do the couples split up? When does the abuse decrease? *Violence and Victims, 11,* 371-92.

Jacobson, N. S., & Gurman, A. S. (1995). *Clinical handbook of couple therapy.* New York: Guilford.

Jacobson, N. S., & Margolin, G. (1979). *Marital therapy: Strategies based on social learning and behavior exchange principles.* New York: Brunner/Mazel.

Jenkins, K. W. (1992). Religion and families. In S. J. Bahr (Ed.), *Family research: A sixty year review, 1930-1990* (Vol 1., pp. 235-288). New York: Lexington Books.

Jensen, J. P., & Bergin, A. E. (1988). Mental health values of professional therapists: A national interdisciplinary survey. *Professional Psychology: Research and Practice, 19,* 290-297.

Johnson, C. A., Stanley, S. M., Glenn, N. D., Amato, P. A., Nock, S. L., Markman, H. J. (2002). *Marriage in Oklahoma: 2001 baseline statewide survey on marriage and divorce.* Oklahoma City: Oklahoma Department of Human Services.

Johnson, S. M., & Greenberg, L. S. (1985). Emotionally focused couples therapy: An outcome study. *Journal of Marital and Family Therapy, 11,* 313-317.

Jung, C. (1933). *Modern man in search of soul.* New York: Harcourt Brace Jovanovich.

Kaplan, H. B., Burch, N. R., Bloom, S. W. (1964). Psychological covariation in small peer groups. In *Psychological Approaches to Social Behavior,* ed. Liederman, P. H., & Shapiro, D., pp. 21-43. Stanford, CA: Stanford University Press.

Karasu, T. (1999). Spiritual psychotherapy. *American Journal of Psychotherapy, 53,* 142-162.

Kelly, E. L., & Conley, J. J. (1987). Personality and compatibility: A prospective analysis of marital stability and marital satisfaction. *Journal of Personality and Social Psychology, 52,* 27-40.

Kennedy, J. E. (2002). Commentary on "experiments on distant intercessory prayer" in archives of internal medicine. *The Journal of Parapsychology, 66,* 177-182.

Kline, G. H., Stanley, S. M., Markman, H. J., Olmos-Gallo, A. P., St. Peters, M., Whitton, S. W., & Prado, L. M. (2004). Timing is everything: Pre-engagement cohabitation and increased risk for poor marital outcomes. *Journal of Family Psychology, 18*(2), 311-318.

Koenig, H. G. (1997). *Is religion good for your health? The effects of religion on physical and mental health.* New York: Haworth Pastoral Press.

Koenig, H. G. (Ed.). (1998). *Handbook of religion and mental health.* San Diego, CA: Academic Press.

Koenig, H. G. (2003). The healing power of prayer. *Christian Counseling Today, 11*(4), 24-26.

Koenig, H. G., & Cohen, H. J. (Eds.). (2002). *The link between religion and health: Psychoneuroimmuniology and the faith factor.* Oxford, England: Oxford University Press.

Koenig, H. G., & Larson, D. B. (2001). Religion and mental health: Evidence for an association. *International Review of Psychiatry, 13,* 67-78.

Koenig, H. G., McCullough, M., & Larson, D. B. (2001). *Handbook of religion and health: A century of research reviewed.* New York: Oxford University Press.

Kollar, C. (1997). *Solution-focused pastoral counseling.* Grand Rapids, MI: Zondervan.

Krokoff, L. J., Gottman, J. M., & Hass, S. D. (1989). Validation of a global rapid couples interaction scoring system. *Behavioral Assessment, 11,* 65-79.

Kroll, J. (1973). A reappraisal of psychiatry in the middle ages. *Archives of General Psychiatry, 29,* 276-283.

Kunzer, M. B. (1987). Marital adjustment of headache sufferers and their spouses. *Journal of Psychosocial Nursing and Mental Health Services, 25,* 12-17.

Ladd, K. L., & Spilka, B. (2002). Inward, outward, and upward: Cognitive aspects of prayer. *Journal for the Scientific Study of Religion, 41*(3), 475-484.

Larson, D. B., Swyers, J. P., & McCullough, M. E. (1998). *Scientific research on spirituality and health: A report based on the Scientific Progress in Spirituality Conferences.* Bethesda, MD: National Institute for Healthcare Research.

Larson, L. E., & Goltz, J. W. (1989). Religious participation and marital commitment. *Review of Religious Research, 30,* 387-400.

Larson, D. B., & Larson, S. S. (2003). Spirituality's potential relevance to physical and emotional health: A brief review of quantitative research. *Journal of Psychology and Theology, 31*(1), 37-51.

Latourette, K. S. (1953). *A history of Christianity.* New York: Harper & Row.

Laub, J. H., Nagin, D. S., & Sampson, R. J. (1998, April). Trajectories of change in criminal offending: Good marriages and the resistance process. *American Sociological Review, 63*(2), 225-238.

Lauer, C. S. (2003). Say a little prayer. *Modern Healthcare, 33*(13), 18-19.

Lawler, M. G. (2001). Changing Catholic models of marriage. *America, 184*(9), 16-18.

Lawler, K. A., & Younger, J. W. (2002). Theobiology: An analysis of spirituality, cardiovascular responses, stress, mood, and physical health. *Journal of Religion and Health, 41*(4), 347-362.

Lawson, E. T., & McCauley, R. N. (1990). *Rethinking religion: Connecting cognition and culture.* Cambridge: University Press.

Leech, K. (1977). *Soul friend: The practice of Christian spirituality.* San Francisco: Harper & Row.

Leedy, P. D., & Ormrod, J. E., (2001). *Practical research: Planning and design* (7th ed.). New Jersey: Prentice-Hall.

Lescher, B. H. (1997, Spring). The professionalization of spiritual direction: Promise and peril. *Listening, 32,* 81-90.

Levenson, R. W., Carstensen, L. L., & Gottman, J. M. (1994). The influence of age and gender on affect, physiology and their interactions: A study of long-term marriages. *Journal of Personality and Social Psychology, 67,* 56-68.

Levenson, R. W., & Gottman, J. M. (1983). Marital interaction: Physiological linkage and affective exchange. *Journal of Personality and Social Psychology, 45,* 587-97.

Levenson, R. W., & Gottman, J. M. (1985). Physiological and affective predictors of change in relationship satisfaction. *Journal of Personality of Social Psychology, 49,* 85-94.

Levin, J. S., & Vanderpool, H. Y. (1989). Is religion therapeutically significant for hypertension? *Social Science and Medicine, 29,* 69-78.

Locke, H. J. (1951). *Predicting adjustment in marriage: A comparison of a divorced and happily married group.* New York: Holt.

Loewenberg, F. M. (1988). *Religion and social work practice in contemporary American society.* New York: Columbia University Press.

Magaletta, P. R., & Brawer, P. A. (1998). Prayer in psychotherapy: A model for its use, ethical considerations, and guidelines for practice. *Journal of Psychology and Theology, 26*(4), 322-330.

Magdol, L., Moffitt, T. E., & Caspi, A. (1998). Hitting without a license: Testing explanations for differences in partner abuse between young adult daters and cohabitors. *Journal of Marriage and the Family, 60,* 41-55.

Mahoney, A., Pargament, K. L., Jewell, T., Swank, A., Scott, E., Emery, E., & Rye, M. (1999). Marriage and the spiritual realm: The role of proximal and distal religious constructs in marital functioning. *Journal of Family Psychology, 13,* 321-338.

Maloney, H. N. (1995). *Psychology and the cross: The early history of Fuller Seminary's School of Psychology.* Pasadena, CA: Fuller Seminary Press.

Markman, H. J. (1981). The prediction of marital distress: A five year follow-up. *Journal of Consulting and Clinical Psychology, 49,* 760-762.

Markman, H., Floyd, F., Stanley, S., & Storaasli, R. (1988). The prevention of marital distress: A longitudinal investigation. *Journal of Consulting and Clinical Psychology, 56,* 210-217.

Markman, H. J., & Hahlweg, K. (1993). The prediction and prevention of marital distress: An international perspective. *Clinical Psychology Review, 13,* 29-43.

Markman, H. J., Renick, M. J., Floyd, F. J., Stanley, S. M., & Clements, M. (1993). Preventing marital distress through communication and conflict management training: A 4- and 5-year follow-up. *Journal of Consulting and Clinical Psychology, 61*(1), 70-77.

Markman, H., Stanley, S., & Blumberg, L. (1994). *Fighting for your marriage.* San Francisco: Jossey-Bass.

Markowski, E. M., & Greenwood, P. D. (1984). Marital adjustment as a correlate of social interest. *Individual Psychology Journal of Adlerian theory, Research and Practice, 40,* 300-308.

McCullough, M. E., Hoyt, W. T., Larson, D. B., Koenig, H. G., & Thoresen, C. (2000). Religious involvement and mortality: A meta-analytic review. *Health Psychology, 19,* 211-222.

McDowell, J., & Stewart, D. (1983). *Handbook of today's religions.* San Bernardino, CA: Here's Life.

McLanahan, S. (2000). Family, state, and child well-being. *Annual Review of Sociology, 26*(1), 703-706.

McMinn, M. R. (1996). *Psychology, theology, and spirituality in Christian counseling.* Wheaton, IL: Tyndale House.

Meredith, W. H., Abbott, D. A., & Adams, S. L. (1986). Family violence: Its relation to marital and parental satisfaction and family strengths. *Journal of Family Violence, 1,* 299-305.

Miller, J. J., Fletcher, K., & Kabat-Zinn, J. (1995). Three-year follow-up and clinical implications of mindfulness meditation-based stress reduction intervention in the treatment of anxiety disorders. *General Hospital Psychiatry, 17,* 192-200.

Miller, W. R., & Thoresen, C. E. (2003). Spirituality, religion, and health: An emerging research field. *American Psychologist, 58*(1), 24-35.

Moller, A. T., & Van Zyl, P. D. (1991). Relationship beliefs, interpersonal perception, and marital adjustment. *Journal of Clinical Psychology, 47*(1), 28-33.

Montoya, R. M., Horton, R. S. (2004). On the importance of cognitive evaluation as a determinant of interpersonal attraction. *Journal of Personality and Social Psychology, 86*(5), 696-712.

Moon, G. (1994, Winter). Spiritual directors, Christian counselors: Where do they overlap? *Christian Counseling Today,* 29-33.

Nichols, M.P., & Schwartz, R.C. (2004). Family therapy concepts and methods (6th edition). Boston: Pearson Education.

Nouwen, H. (1972). *The wounded healer: Ministry in contemporary society.* Garden City, NY: Doubleday.

Oliver, G., Hasz, M., & Richburg, M. (1997). *Promoting change through brief therapy in Christian counseling.* Wheaton, IL: Tyndale.

Omartian, S. (2000). Welcome to Stormie Omartian.com. Retrieved June 18, 2004, from http://www.stormieomartian.com/

Omartian, S. (2004a). *The power of a praying husband: Book of prayers.* Eugene, OR: Harvest House.

Omartian, S. (2004b). *The power of a praying wife: Book of prayers.* Eugene, OR: Harvest House.

Omartian, S., & Hayford, J. (2003). *The power of praying together.* Eugene, OR: Harvest House.

PASS Release 2002. (2002, May 2). *NCSS Statistical Software.* Kaysville, Utah: Author.

Pike, P. L., McMinn, M. R., & Campbell, C. D. (1997). Market and mission. *Journal of Psychology and Theology, 25,* 278-283.

Plante, T. G., & Sherman, A. C. (Eds.), (2001). *Faith and health: Psychological perspectives.* New York: Guilford Press.

Poloma, M. M., & Pendleton, B. F. (1991). The effects of prayer experiences on measures of general well-being. *Journal of Psychology and Theology, 19,* 71-83.

Powell, L. H., Shahabi, L., & Thoresen, C. E. (2003). Religion and spirituality: Linkages to physical health. *American Psychologist, 58*(1), 36-52.

PREP Inc. (2004). *PREP: State of the art tools for an extraordinary marriage.* Retrieved September 30, 2004, from PREP

Web site: http://www.prepinc.com/main/research_foundation.asp

Princeton Religion Research Center. (1996). *Religion in America.* Princeton, NJ: The Gallup Poll.

Propst, L. R. (1980). The comparative efficacy of religious and nonreligious imagery for the treatment of mild depression in religious individuals. *Cognitive Therapy and Research, 4,* 167-178.

Propst, L. R., Ostrom, R., Watkins, R., Dean, T., & Mashburn, D. (1992). Comparative efficacy of religious and nonreligious cognitive-behavior therapy for the treatment of clinical depression in religious individuals. *Journal of Consulting and Clinical Psychology, 60,* 94-103.

Rank, M. R., & Hirschl, T. A. (1999). The economic risk of childhood in America: Estimating the probability of poverty across the formative years. *Journal of Marriage and the Family, 61*(4), 1058-1067.

Rayburn, C. A. (2001). Theobiology, spirituality, religiousness, and the Wizard of Oz. *Psychology of Religion Newsletter, 26,* 1-11.

Razali, S. M., Hasanah, C. L., Aminah, K., & Subramaniam, M. (1998). Religious—sociocultural psychotherapy in patients with anxiety and depression. *Australian & New Zealand Journal of Psychiatry, 32,* 867-872.

Richards, P. S., & Bergin, A. E. (1997). *A spiritual strategy for counseling and psychotherapy.* Washington, DC: American Psychological Association.

Richards, P. S., & Potts, R. W. (1995). Using spiritual interventions in psychotherapy: Practices, successes, failures, and ethical concerns of Mormon psychotherapists. *Professional Psychology: Research and Practice, 26*(2), 163-170.

Ripley, J. S., & Worthington, E. L., Jr. (1998). What the journals reveal about Christian marital counseling: An inadequate (but emerging) scientific base. *Marriage and Family: A Christian Journal, 1,* 375-396.

Ripley, J. S., Worthington, E. L., Jr., & Berry, J. W. (2001). The effects of religiosity on preferences and expectations for marital therapy among married Christians. *The American Journal of Family Therapy, 29,* 39-58.

Ross, C. E., & Mirowsky, J. (1999, November). Parental divorce, life-course disruption, and adult depression. *Journal of Marriage and the Family, 61*(4), 1034-1045.

Ruffing, J. (2000). *Spiritual direction: Beyond the beginnings.* New York: Paulist Press.

Saluter, A. F. (1996). *Marital status and living arrangements: March 1994.* U.S. Bureau of the Census, March 1996; Series P20-484.

Sanders, R. K. (1997). *Christian counseling ethics: A handbook for therapists, pastors, and counselors.* Downers Grove, IL: InterVarsity Press.

Sanua, V. D. (1969). Religion, mental health, and personality: A review of empirical studies. *American Journal of Psychiatry, 125,* 1203-1213.

Schaap, C. (1982). *Communication and adjustment in marriage.* The Netherlands: Swets & Feitlinger.

Schilling, E. A., Baucom, D. H., Burnett, C. K., Allen, E. S., & Ragland, L. (2003). Altering the course of marriage: The effect of PREP communication skills acquisition on couples' risk of becoming martially distressed. *Journal of Family Psychology, **17***(1), 41-53.

Shadish, W. R., Montgomery, L. M., Wilson, P., Wilson, M. R., Bright, I., & Okwumabua, T. (1993). Effects of family and marital psychotherapies: A meta-analysis. *Journal of Consulting and Clinical Psychology, **61***(6), 992-1002.

Shafranske, E. P. (Ed.). (1996). **Religion and the clinical practice of psychology.** Washington, DC: American Psychological Association.

Sher, T. G., & Baucom, D. H. (1993). Marital communication: Differences among martially distressed, depressed, and nondistressed-nondepressed couples. *Journal of Family Psychology, **7***(1), 148-53.

Smolen, R. C., Spiegel, D. A., & Martin, C. J. (1986). Patterns of marital interaction associated with marital dissatisfaction and depression. *Journal of Behavior Therapy and Experimental Psychiatry, **17**,* 261-266.

Spanier, G. B. (1976). Measuring dyadic adjustment: New scales for assessing the quality of marriage and similar dyads. *Journal of Marriage and the Family, **38**,* 15-28.

Spanier, G. B. (1979). The measurement of marital quality. *Journal of Marriage and the Family, 43,* 825-839.

Spanier, G. B. (1998). *Dyadic adjustment scale (DAS) Computer program.* Toronto, Canda: Multi-Health Systems.

Spanier, G. B. (2004). *Dyadic adjustment scale (DAS): User's Manual.* Toronto, Canada: Multi-Health Systems.

Spanier, G. B., & Filsinger, E. E. (1983). The dyadic adjustment scale. In E. E. Filsinger (Ed.), *Marriage and family assessment: A sourcebook in family therapy,* (pp. 34-47). Beverly Hills, CA: Sage.

SPASS (2002, May 2). *Statistical Power and Analysis Software.* Kaysville, UT: NCSS Statistical Software.

Sperry, L. (2003). Integrating spiritual direction functions in the practice of psychotherapy. *Journal of Psychology and Theology, 31*(1), 3-13.

Sprenkle, D. H., & Moon, S. M. (Eds.). (1996). *Research methods in family therapy.* New York: The Guilford Press.

Stairs, J. (2000). *Listening for the soul: Pastoral care and spiritual direction.* Minneapolis: Fortress.

Stanley, S. M. (1986). *Commitment and the maintenance and enhancement of relationships.* Unpublished doctoral dissertation, University of Denver, Denver.

Stanley, S. (1997). What's important in premarital counseling? *Marriage and Family: A Christian Journal, 1,* 51-60.

Stanley, S. (2003). Strengthening marriages in a skeptical culture: Issues and opportunities. *Journal of Psychology and Theology, 31*(3), 224-230.

Stanley, S. (2004, May). *The benefits of a healthy marriage.* Paper presented at the Committee on Finance, Subcommittee on Social Security and Family Policy United States Senate, Washington, D. C.

Stanley, S. M., & Markman, H. J. (1992). Assessing commitment in personal relationships. *Journal of Marriage and the Family, 54,* 595-608.

Stanley, S. M., & Markman, H. J. (1998). *Acting on what we know: The hope of prevention.* Paper presented at the Family Impact Seminar, Washington D. C.

Stanley, S. M., Markman, H. J., Prado, L. M., Olmos-Gallo, P. A., Tonelli, L., St. Peters, M., Leber, B. D., Bobulinski, M., Cordova, A., & Whitton, S. (2001). Short term effects of premarital training in a religious, community based sample. *Family Relations, 50,* 67-76.

Stanley, S., Trathen, D., McCain, S., & Bryan, M. (1998). *A lasting promise: A Christian guide to fighting for your marriage.* San Francisco: Jossey-Bass.

Stanton, G. T. (1997). *Why marriage matters: Reasons to believe in marriage in postmodern society.* Colorado Springs, CO: Pinon Press.

Statistical Package for the Social Sciences. (2003). SPSS Graduate Pack, Release 12.0 for Windows [Computer Program]. Chicago: SPSS.

Steere, D. (1997). *Spiritual presence in psychotherapy: A guide for caregivers.* New York: Brunner/Mazel.

Stein, S. J., Girodo, M., & Dotzenroth, S. (1982). The interrelationships and reliability of a multilevel behavior-based assessment package for distressed couples. *Journal of Behavioral Assessment, 4,* 343-360.

Strachey, J. (Ed.). (1962). *Standard edition of the complete psychological works of Sigmund Freud.* London: Hogarth Press, 1962.

Stone, H. (1999). Pastoral counseling and the changing times. *Journal of Pastoral Care, 53,* 119-127.

Tan, S. Y. (1994). Ethical considerations in religious psychotherapy: Potential pitfalls and unique resources. *Journal of Psychology and Theology, 22*(4), 389-394.

Tan, S. Y. (2003). Integrating spiritual direction into psychotherapy: Ethical issues and guidelines. *Journal of Psychology and Theology, 31*(1), 14-23.

Taubes, T. (1998). Healthy avenues of the mind: Psychological theory building and the influence of religion during the era of moral treatment. *American Journal of Psychiatry, 155,* 1001-1008.

Tepper, L., Rogers, S. A., Coleman, E. M., & Maloney, H. N. (2001). The prevalence of religious coping among persons with persistent mental illness. *Psychiatric Services, 52*(5), 660-665.

The Gottman Institute, Inc. (2004). *Researching and restoring relationships.* Retrieved September 30, 2004, from The Gottman Institute Web site: http://www.gottman.com/

Thompson, T., & Dockens, III., W. S. (1975). *Applications in behavior modification.* New York: Academic Press.

Thomson, E., & Colella, U. (1992). Cohabitation and marital stability: Quality or commitment? *Journal of Marriage and the Family, 54,* 259-67.

Thoresen, C. E. (1999). Spirituality and health: Is there a relationship? *Journal of Health Psychology, 4,* 291-300.

Thornton, M. (1984). *Spiritual direction.* New York: Cowley.

Ting-Toomey, S. (1983). An analysis of verbal communication patterns in high and low marital adjustment groups. *Human Communication Research, 9,* 306-319.

U.S. Census Bureau. (2000). *Census 2000 briefs and special reports.* Retrieved September 30, 2004, from http://www.census.gov/population/www/cen2000/briefs.html

Vandewater, E. A. & Lansford, J. E. (1998). Influences of family structure and parental conflict on children's well-being. *Family Relations, 47*(4), 323-330.

Vincent, J. P. (Ed.). (1980). *Advances in family intervention, assessment, and theory.* Greenwich, CT: JAI Press.

Wallerstein, J. (1991). The long-term effects of divorce on children: A review. *Journal of the American Academy of Child and Adolescent Psychiatry, 30,* 349-360.

Wallerstein, J. (1995). *The good marriage: How and why love lasts.* Boston: Houghton Mifflin.

Wallerstein, J. S. (2000). *The unexpected legacy of divorce: A 25-year landmark study.* New York: Hyperion.

Wallerstein, J. S., & Lewis, J. M. (2004). The unexpected legacy of divorce: Report of a 25-year study. *Psychoanalytic Psychology, 21*(3), 353-70.

Walsh, V. L., Baucom, D. H., Tyler, S., & Sayers, S. L. (1993). Impact of message valence, focus, expressive style, and gender on communication patterns among martially distressed couples. *Journal of Family Psychology, 7*(2), 163-75.

Weiss, R. L., (1980). Strategic behavioral marital therapy: Toward a model for assessment and intervention. In J. P. Vincent (Ed.). *Advances in family intervention, assessment, and theory* (Vol. 1, pp. 229-271). Greenwich, CT: JAI Press.

Weiss, R. L., & Tolman, A. O. (1990). The marital interaction coding system—global (MICS-G): A global comparison to the MICS. *Behavioral Assessment, 12,* 271-294.

Wellness and divorce. (2000). *Ardell Wellness Report, 56,* 3-5.

Westfield, J. (2001). Spiritual issues in counseling: Clients beliefs and preferences. *Journal of Counseling Psychology, 48,* 61-71.

Wilson, J., & Musick, M. (1996). Religion and marital dependency. *Journal for the Scientific Study of Religion, 35,* 30-40.

Wilson, M. R., & Filsinger, E. E. (1986). Religiosity and marital adjustment: Multidimensional interrelationships. *Journal of Marriage and the Family, 48,* 148-151.

Wimberly, J. D. (1998). An outcome study of integrative couples therapy delivered in a group format (Doctoral dissertation, University of Montana, 1997). *Dissertation Abstracts International: Section B: The Sciences & Engineering, 58(12-B),* 6832.

Wise, C. (1983). *Pastoral psychotherapy: Theory and practice.* New York: Jason Aronson.

Worthington, E. L., Jr. (1986). Religious counseling: A review of published empirical research. *Journal of Counseling and Development, 64,* 421-431.

Worthington, E. L., Jr. (1990). Marriage counseling: A Christian approach to counseling couples. *Counseling and Values, 35,* 3-15.

Worthington, E. L., Jr., Kurusu, T. A., McCullough, M. E., & Sandage, S. J. (1996). Empirical research on religion and psychotherapeutic processes and outcomes: A 10-year review and research prospectus. *Psychological Bulletin, 119*(3), 448-487.

Younggren, J. N. (1993). Ethical issues in religious psychotherapy. *Register Report, 19*(4), 1-8.

Zilboorg, G. (1941). *Freud and religion: A restatement of an old controversy.* Westminster, MD: Newman Press.

Appendix A

PARTICIPANT DEMOGRAPHIC INFORMATION

Today's Date _____ Couple I.D. _____

[ ] Female   [ ] Male   Age _____

City of Residence _____   State _____

Are you currently employed outside your home?

    [ ] Yes   [ ] No

    If yes, how many hours per week do you usually work? _____

Education (years completed) _____

Are you currently in any form of psychotherapy or counseling?

    [ ] Yes   [ ] No

    If yes, please check one or more:

        [ ] Individual Therapy   [ ] Marital Therapy   [ ] Other

Please check one: [ ] Protestant   [ ] Catholic

Phone Number (_____) _____   E-Mail _____

Appendix B

An Experiment in Marital Satisfaction

Prayer Tracking Journal & Instructions

Couple ID _____

[ ] Male

[ ] Female

Research Participant,

Thank you for volunteering to participate in this study of prayer. This is not meant as a substitute for marital therapy, rather a study to determine if prayer can improve couples' levels of satisfaction with their relationship. You and your spouse have each taken the Dyadic Adjustment Scale (DAS). You have also each been given a Prayer Booklet by Stormie Omartian. Men should use the one entitled The Power of a Praying Husband and women should use the one entitled The Power of a Praying Wife. Now we would like you to begin praying these prayers each day for the next 30 days.

Two prayers are assigned for you to pray each day, at some time during the day. The prayers are identified on the next pages by the page number in your Omartian Prayer Booklet.

Please take a few moments to recite each prayer out loud, one prayer in the morning and another prayer in the evening. Think carefully about the words you are praying and try to recall them during the course of your day. In order to help you remember to recite the prayers and to help us know that you have completed the prayers, place a check in the "Check" column of this journal after you have recited it.

If you have any questions about the instructions, please call the office of Family Counseling Associates at (317) 585-1060 or Toll-Free (888) 701-1060 and speak to one of the Prayer Study Research Assistants.

You will be contacted each week with a brief phone call reminder about the prayers and then again in 30 days to turn in this Prayer Tracking Journal and re-take the Dyadic Adjustment Scale (DAS) test.

On the next page you will find step-by-step instructions for your task in this research study. Your results can only be considered in this important study if you complete the prayers in the manner prescribed. Please do your best to make this a part of your daily routine. If you should miss a prayer go ahead and make it up on another day and note the date when you actually prayed the prayer in the date column of this journal.

Identifying information will remain confidential in this study. Your results will be coded so that no one will have access to your name(s), only the data results. At the conclusion of this study the results will be collected, analyzed, and interpreted. You will receive a written synopsis of those results by mail.

Thank you again for participating in this research study about prayer and marriage. It is our hope that you will find this a rewarding experience and one that makes a difference in your marriage.

Gratefully,
Timothy A. Heck

Appendix C

Prayer Tracking Journal

STEP-BY-STEP INSTRUCTIONS

1. Pray two (2) prayers each day, Morning (am) and Evening (pm).
2. You do not have to pray the prayer with your spouse, but you are welcome to do so, if you would like.
3. Pray the prayer listed on the page number in this Journal.
4. Please pray the prayer out loud, even if you are alone.
5. Put the date in the second column on this Journal.
6. Please just put a check in the third column of this Journal indicating that you read the prayer.
7. Think about the prayer during the day.
8. You will be returning this Prayer Tracking Journal to the research team after you complete the 30 days of prayer.
9. In 30 days you will be contacted by our research team to arrange a time to return your Prayer Tracking Journal and take the DAS Test again.
10. Contact the Research Team at (317) 585-1060 or Toll-Free outside the Indianapolis area.

Appendix D

An Experiment in Marital Satisfaction

A RESEARCH STUDY

Thought for the Day Tracking
Journal & Instructions

Thought for the Day Tracking Journal & Instructions

Couple ID _____

[ ] Male

[ ] Female

Research Participant,

    Thank you for volunteering to participate in this study of marital satisfaction. This is not meant as a substitute for marital therapy, rather a study to determine if daily thoughts can improve couples' levels of satisfaction with their relationship. You and your spouse have each taken the Dyadic Adjustment Scale (DAS). Now we would like you to begin reading through these daily thoughts each day for the next 30 days.

    Please take a few moments to recite each thought for the day out loud, once in the morning and again in the evening. Think carefully about the words and try to recall them during the course of your day. In order to help you remember to and to help us know that you have completed the readings, place a check in the "Check" column of this journal after you have recited it.

    If you have any questions about the instructions, please call the office of Family Counseling Associates at (317) 585-1060 or Toll-Free (888) 701-1060 and speak to one of the Marital Satisfaction Study Research Assistants.

    You will be contacted each week with a brief phone call reminder about the readings and then again in 30 days to turn in this Thought for the Day Tracking Journal and re-take the Dyadic Adjustment Scale (DAS) test.

    On the next page you will find step-by-step instructions for your task in this research study. Please do your best to make this a part of your daily routine. If you should miss a reading go ahead and make it up on another day and note the date when you actually read it in the date column of this journal.

Identifying information will remain confidential in this study. Your results will be coded so that no one will have access to your name(s), only the data results. At the conclusion of this study the results will be collected, analyzed, and interpreted. You will receive a written synopsis of those results by mail.

Thank you again for participating in this research study about interventions to improve marital satisfaction. It is our hope that you will find this a rewarding experience and one that makes a difference in your marriage.

Gratefully,

Timothy A. Heck

Thought for the Day Tracking Journal

STEP-BY-STEP INSTRUCTIONS

1. Recite one thought for the day two times each day, Morning (am) and Evening (pm).
2. You do not have to read the thought for the day with your spouse, but you are welcome to do so, if you would like.
3. Please recite the thought for the day out loud, even if you are alone.
4. Put the date in the second column on this Journal.
5. Please just put a check in the third column of this Journal indicating that you read the thought.
6. Think about the thought during the day.
7. You will be returning this Thought for the Day Tracking Journal to the research team after you complete the 30 days.
8. In 30 days you will be contacted by our research team to arrange a time to return your Thought for the Day Tracking Journal and take the DAS Test again.
9. Contact the Research Team at (317) 585-1060 or Toll-Free outside the Indianapolis area (888) 701-1060 with any questions.

Thank you for participating in this study to explore the effect certain thoughts for your spouse can have on satisfaction in your marriage!

Dr. Timothy Heck is available for speaking engagements, including a brief talk, workshops, retreats and conferences. For more information about his research or to schedule him to speak at your event, please contact us at:

Liturgies, P.C.

Liturgies.org

info@liturgies.org

P.O. Box 503464

Indianapolis, IN 46250

www.ingramcontent.com/pod-product-compliance
Lightning Source LLC
Chambersburg PA
CBHW051356290426
44108CB00015B/2033